The Long Way Home

a story of hope and survival by

Shauna Joas

The Long Way Home

Shauna Joas

ISBN: 978-1-66787-360-2

Prelude

The doorbell rings. Who could possibly be stopping by at this time of night? In this day and age, no one just stops by anymore without a text warning or a phone call. If it was earlier in the evening, it could be a neighbor friend looking to play. It is possible it is a solicitor or some sales call, but those have been extremely rare over the past few years. My anxiety, which had been building all evening, reaches the climax as our son yells, "It's the police!".

Chapter 1

In March in Minnesota, the average temperature is typically thirty-five degrees. In 2016, March had a warm stretch of temperatures well above normal. This translated to an early start to the outdoor bicycling season. Today on March 8, it was going to reach the mid-sixties. My husband, Bryan, was ecstatic to get off his indoor trainer and out of the car to be able to ride his bike to work. He normally takes the opportunity to ride to and from work whenever the weather permits. This allows him to be able to get rides in without sacrificing any other time commitments. His ride to work is eight miles. It takes about thirty-five minutes to bike it. He casually rides to work so he doesn't get too sweaty or dirty, since there is no shower at his work. However, on his way home, he typically would take a long route home. Bryan's common bike commute routine was drastically interrupted this evening. We couldn't know that taking advantage of this unseasonably beautiful weather would forever alter our family's fate.

It was damp in the morning, so Bryan was waiting for the roads to dry before leaving for work. Typically, Bryan left around 7:15 a.m. to get to work, change clothes, and start his day at 8:00 a.m., but he was still in the entryway at 8:00 a.m. getting his riding gear on. I was running late, as usual, trying to get the kids and myself out the door. We fortunately all had the same destination of Red Pine Elementary. This was where I taught kindergarten. Griffin was in fourth grade and Elyse was in second. Bryan was usually gone before our mad scramble out the door began, but he was blocking the door today. Actually, I was annoyed that he was in our way, so we rushed by him and out the door without even saying goodbye. *Why hadn't I said goodbye?* Unknown to me, this was going to be the last time I saw "my Bryan" for many weeks.

It was another ordinary day in my kindergarten classroom with the high energy of five- and six-year-olds. At 3:30 p.m., Bryan sent me an email: "The ride in was ok. A little damp, but I didn't get wet. I was actually too warm. I am going to leave in the next fifteen minutes or so." I didn't read the email until after school, which was around 4:00 p.m., so I didn't respond since he would have already been on his bike and not gotten the message. Since daylight savings hadn't started, in order to get a long ride in and not get caught in the dark, he needed to leave work early. He was excited to get a jump start on his training for the upcoming one-hundred-ten-mile gravel road race he had signed up for at the beginning of June in South Dakota. Bryan would generally ride forty to fifty miles on his way home from work on his training days, which he called taking the "long way" home. This took between two or three hours, making his estimated time of arrival home between 6:30 to 7:30 p.m.

It was going to be busy after school that day. I had to take Griffin, who was ten, to his first lacrosse practice of the season. Bryan often volunteered to help coach whenever there was a need. He also usually took Griffin to lacrosse because he helped coach. However, this year there was a requirement to go through an online training course before you were allowed to interact with the team so, because he hadn't completed his online coaching training yet, he couldn't coach today. He decided to go for a ride instead. Griffin was so excited for practice. Out of all the sports he participated in (football, baseball, soccer, basketball, and hockey), lacrosse was his favorite. He had his equipment ready to go the night before. Luckily, it was only an hour long practice because Elyse, who was eight, had to tag along and wasn't too happy about it. I sat with some of the dads of Griffin's friends and chatted. They weren't surprised that Bryan wasn't there but out biking in this beautiful weather. Elyse sat next to me playing on her iPad since there were no little sisters to run around with like there normally were at other sport practices such as hockey. She didn't complain too much. The time passed by quickly.

Since we had busy schedules, I did meal planning for the week to help with time management and to ensure we had homemade meals. Tonight's meal was spaghetti. So as soon as we got home, I started boiling the water for the noodles and browning the meat. Whether we sat down to eat dinner together or not was dependent on our schedules. Did one of the kids have a practice, game, or lesson? Was there a meeting I had to go to? But always when Bryan's training schedule called for a long ride home, we knew to eat without him. He knew there would be a leftover plate to heat up when he got home.

As I made dinner, my parents called to tell me they had arrived in Nashville, Tennessee. They were on their way to Florida for three weeks. My mom told me about the hotel they were staying in, The Gaylord Opryland. It sounded extravagant with the stained glass ceiling and waterfall. They had just finished unpacking their bags and were headed down to happy hour.

I wasn't paying attention to the time as Elyse, Griffin, and I sat down to eat dinner. We usually began our dinner conversation with the kids telling their highs and lows of the day.

Griffin was eager to go first. "Guess what my high was?"

"Hmmm, let me guess? Math class?" I joked.

"NOOO. It was lacrosse practice."

"I figured that it would be. It looked like you were having a lot of fun out there with your friends."

"I scored seven goals. I think we are going to have a good team this year."

"Do you have a low?" I asked.

"Nope. I can't think of anything."

"OK. Elyse, what was your high and low of the day?"

"My low was sitting at Griffin's lacrosse practice. It was so boring."

"I know it wasn't fun for you, but you can't stay home by yourself yet."

"But my high was lunch and recess. We had Italian dunkers, which are my favorite, and I got to go on the tire swing with Emma."

"It sounds like you had a good time."

Elyse asked, "Mom, what was your high and low for the day?"

"Looking for snorkeling excursions for when we go to Puerto Vallarta for Spring Break was my high."

Both kids talked over each other.

"Really?"

"That would be so cool!"

"I want to do that."

Elyse kept saying, "Please, please, please!"

"Does anyone want to hear my low?"

"Sure," Griffin said.

"My low will be cleaning up after dinner," I said, laughing.

When we were done with dinner, the kids brought their plates to the sink, and I began to clean up. I realized that it was getting dark and Bryan wasn't home yet. That was not normal. I looked at the clock. It was 6:45 p.m. If he'd left at 3:45 p.m., he would have been home by now.

Soon, it was completely dark. There was something not right. *Bryan always is home before dark. Where was he?* I tried not to panic. *I'm sure he'll walk through the door any minute.* Whenever he was late, I would get kind of irritated, especially on Saturdays or Sundays when he would go for one-hundred-mile rides and be gone for six or seven hours. But then I'd think, *What if?* As soon as I started thinking about the "what if," Bryan would walk through the door with some explanation and wonder why I was worried or mad. *Maybe he got held up at work and didn't get out for the ride until later. Maybe he underestimated the time. Maybe he had gotten a flat tire.*

I called him, but there was no answer. Bryan customarily didn't answer his phone while he was riding, so I wasn't surprised. I tried texting him: "Are you almost home?" No response. "Where are you?" I was trying to remain calm and not worry the kids, so I told them to go upstairs and take baths.

It was now 7:00 p.m. The panic was starting to kick in, and my heart was beating a little faster. I called and texted Bryan a few more times. Nothing. My mind was racing through all the scenarios in my head . . . *He got a flat tire, his phone died, OR, a rider's wife's worst nightmare: he was in an accident. What should I do? If I call the police, what would I say?* I had no idea what route Bryan took. He picked his routes based on the weather, which direction the wind was blowing, and what roads had good shoulders and not a lot of traffic.

No, I am not going to freak out. Take a deep breath. Bryan is an experienced rider. He is fine.

Not knowing what else to do, I started my nightly routine a bit early, about one and a half hours early. I thought if I could keep things normal, then everything would be fine. The kids were finishing up their baths as I went upstairs to our bedroom and laid out my workout clothes so that, when I got up at 4:45 a.m., I could get dressed quickly and quietly to get to the gym by 5:00 a.m. Next, I put my school clothes in order. Finally, I put on my pajamas. I glanced at the clock—7:40 p.m.—and went into our bathroom and shut the door. Bryan should have been home an hour or two ago. *OK, breathe. Think. After I brush my teeth, if Bryan isn't home yet, I am going to have to call the police. I have procrastinated long enough. There has to be something wrong. I don't want the kids to hear when I call the police. I will have them go get a bedtime snack.* I opened the bathroom door and yelled down the hall, "When you are done getting your pajamas on, go downstairs and get a bedtime snack. I will be down in a few minutes."

"OK, Mom," they both answered.

I shut the door. I needed just a little more time before I called the police because, once I called the police, I would be admitting that something was wrong. I turned on the water, started my electric toothbrush, and hoped that, when I was done brushing my teeth, Bryan would be home.

Instead, we had an unexpected visitor ringing the doorbell. Griffin burst through the bathroom door. "Mom!" he screamed. "MOM, the police are here!"

Chapter 2

"Griffin, that is not funny," I snapped. "This is not a joke."

"I'm not lying," he stammered as he began to cry.

I turned to look into eyes I had never seen before. They were terror filled and brimming with tears. My poor, sensitive, kindhearted baby had to answer the door to find the police there.

"They told me to come and get you," he continued.

The worst had happened. The fear I had been trying to push down suddenly erupted to the surface. Anxiety pulsed through my core and settled like an elephant on my chest. I dropped my toothbrush and ran past Griffin to the stairs. I flew down them, my feet barely touching. I could see the shadows of the officers through the glass storm door. They really were there. Elyse and Griffin followed just as quickly and hid behind me. I wished I could protect them from what we might hear, but I couldn't ignore the door. I had to open it.

As I reached for the door, my body began to shake uncontrollably, my teeth chattering. All I could hear was my heart beating. My chest felt like it would explode. Through the storm door, I saw two female police officers.

They both seemed around my age. Their faces and body language told me that something was very wrong.

Time came to an abrupt halt. My feet felt cemented to the floor. NO, NO, NO! Bryan was supposed to be walking through the door. I shouldn't be staring at two police officers standing at my front door. *Now I won't have to call the police. They already found me.* The dreadful "knock on the door" that only happened in the movies or TV was happening to me. *This can't be real. But it is. What are they going to tell me?* It was like an out-of-body experience. I didn't cry. I didn't scream. My body started trembling uncontrollably; I could barely stand. Without even thinking, my shaking hand reached out to push open the storm door.

The cool air hit me as the first officer spoke. "Hello, I'm Sergeant Wegner," she said, "and this is my partner, Sergeant Anselment." She nodded to the woman next to her. "Do you know Bryan Joas?"

"Yes, he's my husband."

"Can you please step outside?"

I cautiously stepped out onto the landing. The storm door closed behind me. Yet, I could still hear Griffin's sobs. Griffin, my emotional child, wore his heart on his sleeve. I turned back to look through the door. I saw Griffin sitting on the stairs hunched over with his hands over his face. Elyse, my strong-willed, independent child, looked back and forth between Griffin and me. Her eight-year-old brain was trying to process what was happening.

"Bryan has been in an accident. It was a hit and run," said Sergeant Wegner quietly. "He was airlifted to North Memorial Hospital. We don't know any more details than that."

A sudden fog settled over me. I stood there staring and nodding my head. I was hearing what was being said, but it had to go through thick muddy water to get to my ears. I had never heard of North Memorial. *Where the hell is North Memorial? How would I get there? Why did they take him there? I have to get to Bryan. Who's going to watch Griffin and Elyse? What happened?*

Sergeant Wegner continued, "You need to go to the hospital now. Do you have any family that can drive you there? I think you should have someone drive you there."

"No. My family all lives in Wisconsin." *Who can take me to the hospital? Who could get here the quickest?* "You can go to Carmen's house. Maybe she can take me," I said as I pointed to the house next door.

"OK. I will go ask her," Sergeant Wegner said and headed across the yard to Carmen's.

"Why don't you change out of your pajamas and get dressed," Sergeant Anselment told me.

I looked down. I forgot I was in my pajamas. "OK." I stumbled back inside. Sergeant Anselment followed.

Griffin and Elyse were sitting on the stairs. Griffin was bawling, and Elyse was still showing no emotion. As a mom, you know that your children can feel your fear and will mimic your feelings. I knelt down, put my arms around them, and told them as calmly as I could, "Dad was in an accident and I have to go to the hospital."

Griffin's sobs turned into hysterics. Elyse continued to be stoic; only a few tears pooled in her eyes.

"I have to change out of my pajamas, then I have to leave." I was following the directions the officer had given me. It was the only thing my mind and body could do. "Carmen is going to bring me to the hospital. Someone is going to come and stay with you. You'll be OK."

I started up the stairs to my bedroom. I had tunnel vision. All my brain could focus on was getting to Bryan. Bryan needed me.

Upstairs in my closet, trying to figure out what to wear seemed like an unimaginable task. I couldn't think straight. I just put on the first things

I grabbed. A black pair of sweatpants, a green Summit beer shirt I had won at Cub Foods, and an old black fleece sweatshirt from my former school where I taught. Pretty ugly, but it would do. I was shaking so badly, I could barely get dressed.

While upstairs changing, Sergeant Anselment sat with my kids, hugging them and saying, "Do you ever say prayers?"

"Yes," Griffin and Elyse both replied.

"So, let's pray," Sergeant Anselment said. "Dear God, please give Bryan the strength to pull through. Watch over his family and give them strength. Amen"

"Amen," Griffin and Elyse repeated.

"It's going to be OK. Your dad is in good care," Sergeant Anselment continued.

By the time I got downstairs, Carmen was waiting in the driveway. Saying goodbye to the kids was excruciating. I couldn't imagine what they were thinking. I am very truthful with my kids, so I wasn't going to tell them Bryan was going to be fine. I knew that, if the outcome was anything other than fine, my kids would come back at me with, "You told us Dad would be fine." The last thing I needed was them angry or resentful toward me. I gave them a hug and kiss. "I don't really know what is happening, but I need to get to Dad. I love you both so much."

As I was saying my goodbyes, there was my neighbor, Jill, with her red hair flying behind her, running up the driveway ready to take care of Griffin and Elyse. Jill hugged and reassured me. "I've got the kids. You go be with Bryan." How did she know? I had no idea. I was just relieved that the kids were in safe hands. I jumped in Carmen's white SUV, and we began our journey to the hospital. She reached for my hand in a silent gesture; I knew she had my back.

The drive to the hospital was a blur and seemed to take forever. I couldn't stop shivering. Shock had set in. My mind was numb. Tears still didn't come. I kept thinking, *Bryan will be fine when I get to the hospital. Maybe some road rash and broken bones. Only a couple of years before Bryan crashed in a race that broke his bike in two and had a deep gash over his eye. He was stranded at the side of the road for a long time before he was transported back to the start finish area where he received some medical attention. Scary, but he was just fine. Maybe this is just another case like that ...* But it wasn't. If he only needed a few stitches or had some broken bones, why would he have been airlifted to a hospital so far away and not just transported by ambulance?

I needed to snap out of it. This was big, so things needed to be taken care of. Calls needed to be made. I called my parents first. I was sure they were wondering why I was calling, since we had talked not even two hours earlier.

"Mom, Bryan was in an accident."

"What?" she gasped. "Is he OK?"

"I don't know. He was on his bike and was hit. He's been airlifted to the hospital."

"Oh my God! We will come back."

"No, Mom. Don't do that. Just go to Florida." Clearly, I was not comprehending the situation. "Let's just wait until I know more and see how things are. I will call you." I did not want to ruin their trip either.

"Shauna, call as soon as you know anything. You call, no matter what time."

"I will, Mom. Love you."

"I love you, too."

Later I learned that, as soon as my mom got off the phone with me, she turned to my dad and said, "Bryan has been in an accident and airlifted to the hospital. Being airlifted cannot be good. We are going back." Then she went to the front desk to tell them there was a family emergency. They would be leaving in the morning and to please cancel their room for the remaining days.

Next, I needed to call Bryan's dad, Steve. This was a call I dreaded. How would I tell him his son had been in a terrible accident? No parent wants to hear the words, "Something bad has happened to your child." Bryan and his dad had always kept in touch and had a good relationship.

I dialed the number. It seemed like forever before Steve answered. "Hi, Steve."

"Shauna?" he said in a surprised voice because I never called Bryan's parents. Bryan always did.

"Yes, it is me. I don't know how to tell you this, but Bryan has been in a serious bike accident. Do you think you can come right now? I really think you need to."

"Oh NO! What happened?" he stammered.

"All I know is that he was involved in a hit-and-run and was airlifted to North Memorial Hospital."

"Where is that?" he asked.

Questions like this were beyond my comprehension. "I'm not really sure. Carmen is driving me there now. We are following the GPS. It looks like it is near Minneapolis."

"I will get there as soon as I can." It would be an almost two-hour drive ahead of him from Chippewa Falls, Wisconsin.

"OK. Drive safely."

OK, who do I call next? My sister, Erica. She, of course, said she would come right away. She also lived in Chippewa Falls. I told her to wait, since I didn't really know anything yet.

I am going to need a sub for tomorrow. I'll call Kristen, the kindergarten team leader; I'm sure she will do that for me.

Jaleh, my triathlon training partner, happened to text me while I was in the car. She was confirming what we were going to do the next morning. "Swim, bike, run?"

Jaleh and I had met eight years earlier during a 5:30 a.m. fitness class when we were both eight months pregnant with our second children. I got her to start doing triathlons with me, and every Wednesday we would swim, then go to spin class for a half an hour, and finish with a run. In the winter, we would go up to the treadmills and sprint one mile. When the weather was nicer (we were fair weather runners), we would run three miles outside.

I texted her back, "Carmen, my next door neighbor is taking me to the hospital right now. Bryan was in an accident when he was riding home from work."

"Oh my gosh, Shauna. I am sorry. Keep me posted."

With all the calls made, all I could do was pray silently. *Please let him be OK. Please let him be OK.* I had no idea where we were going. I just watched the GPS. It was thirty miles to the hospital. It seemed like we were not even moving. It was the longest ride of my life. I dreaded what was awaiting me at the destination but still couldn't get there fast enough.

Chapter 3

My parents were both retired. My mom, Lou Ann, owned her own dance studio and taught dance for thirty-three years. She taught ballet, tap, and jazz to four-year-olds through adults in our small community, including me, my sister, nieces, Griffin, and Elyse. My dad, Jim, was a branch manager of a bank for seven years and then executive director of the Chippewa Falls YMCA for thirty-one years. My mom always volunteered at school during the day, and since she worked in the evenings, my dad was in charge of taking me to all of my after-school activities. Family was the number one priority for my family. That never changed even as I got older. I am extremely close to both of my parents. They were the first people I would call to tell about the happenings in my life, good or bad. I knew they always had my back.

Bryan's parents had their own challenges. Bryan's mom, Jan, who had provided the majority of the emotional support and was the glue that really kept his family together was suffering from dementia. Bryan's dad, an engineer by trade, was always extremely helpful with physical work and help. He contributed on home improvement projects, car issues, and building custom furniture. He would always drop what he was doing to help with these sorts of issues. Bryan really learned the meaning of hard work from him, but his parents were a team. They would never be as good on their own as they were together. Steve's skills did not appear to translate well to the situation that was unfolding. He was struggling in accepting and dealing with Jan's cognitive decline. Jan's disease also put a strain on Bryan and his sister Gina's relationship. They were never really close, but Jan could not maintain the family dynamics like she did when she was healthy to plan group events such as holiday dinners or vacations. Gina's family was living in Alabama making distance a factor also. It was difficult to expect any support from Gina because of that disconnect.

Chapter 4

Once we got to the hospital, Carmen dropped me off at the emergency room door so she could go park the car. I didn't know what I was going to hear when I entered the ER. *Are they going to tell me I'm too late, that Bryan died?* I somehow managed to walk through the door. My legs were pulsating with fear and weakness. I was still shivering all over. I told the person at the front desk who I was and that I was told that my husband had been airlifted there.

She immediately said, "Follow me." I obeyed her command and followed. Through the swinging doors and down the hall, I followed behind her. Then, as we rounded a corner, there was Bryan on a gurney, surrounded by nurses. As soon as I saw him, everything went into slow motion. Silence. White—all I saw was white. White was everywhere: the walls, the sheets covering him, the floors, the ceiling, his skin color. There was no blood. No outward signs of an accident. It looked as if he were sleeping. In that brief instant, I wanted to fix his helmet hair. He looked like my Bryan, except for the neck brace, the tube down his throat, and the nurses squeezing the bag to give him the breath of life.

A nurse said, "You can give him a kiss."

I leaned over and kissed Bryan's pale, cold forehead. "I love you," I whispered.

"He has a severe pelvic fracture and is bleeding internally. We are taking him to surgery."

Then they whisked him through the swinging doors.

I stood there staring as the doors swung back and forth and finally came to a stop. I didn't know if that would be the last time I would see Bryan. I flashed back to that morning . . . walking right by him and not even saying goodbye. *Why didn't I give him a kiss or even say goodbye? How many times had I done that before and thought nothing of it.* It would haunt me. *Would this be my last memory of him alive?* I made a vow right then—I would never leave without saying goodbye. Not just to Bryan, to anyone.

Chapter 5

Fourteen years earlier, in 2002, I was at a point in my life when I was beginning to wonder if I would ever find that certain someone. There aren't many men who teach at the elementary level, so my chances of meeting a future husband at work were slim. And I was working two other jobs in addition to teaching, so I didn't have a ton of time to date. My friends had set me up on a few blind dates, but those ended after the first date. There was no connection, and I didn't want to waste the little free time I had on something I knew had no future.

Then I joined LifeTime Fitness in Eagan. Maybe my luck would change. On the first day I went to work out, there he was! Ironically, it was someone I had known for almost my entire life.

I was done with my workout and rushing home to get ready for work. I quickly walked past the cardio equipment, and then I stopped and did a double take. Oh my gosh, could that be Bryan Joas, the boy who lived across the street from me in Chippewa Falls practically my whole life? I hadn't seen Bryan in over fifteen years since he and my sister had graduated from high school, but I was almost certain it was him.

Even though it was early in the morning, I called my sister, Erica, who was friends with Bryan when we were growing up. "Do you know where Bryan Joas is living? I am certain I saw him at my new gym this morning. He is so good looking."

"I have no idea. The last I knew, he was living in Wausau, Wisconsin. But what a small world if it was him."

"I know, right?"

A few days later, Erica called back to say that she had run into Bryan's mom, and in fact, he was living in the Twin Cities area and single.

Now I was positive it was him. Would I have the nerve to say hi? I saw him a few more times and told myself to say hi, but every time I was about to, I chickened out. Would he even know me? His family lived kitty-corner from my family, so we had grown up together. Bryan and Erica had been good friends all through school since they were in the same grade, but being that I was four years younger, I had been pretty much invisible.

Bryan was a cute guy, with nice green eyes and dimples, so it made getting up to work out at 5:30 a.m. a little easier. Maybe I could get him to say hi to me? So the stalking began. I would happen to be in the stretching area with a shirt on that said "Leinenkugel's" (hometown brew) as he left the cycling studio, trying to give him some clues.

Finally, one morning when I was on an abdominal machine (the one where you put your arms up like goal posts and twist your hips side to side), Bryan came up to me and said, "You're Shauna."

AWKWARD. Could he have picked a worse time to say hi? I clumsily slipped my arms out of the machine and brought them down by my sides and said, "Yes, and you're Bryan."

We talked for a few minutes about the coincidence that we were both at the Eagan LifeTime Fitness at 5:30 a.m. He told me that the place he worked at was right down the road. He lived thirty minutes north and wanted to beat the morning rush hour. I told him that I was living and teaching in Eagan. We both had to get to work. So the conversation came to an end with "goodbye" and "see you around."

After that initial conversation, we began to say hello and make small talk if we would see each other. Every morning, I would try to look my best in the hopes that I would see him. It was like I was back in middle school hoping to see my crush in the hallway.

A few weeks after that first "hello," he asked, "Would you be interested in coming to a Packer/Viking party at my house? I've invited some friends from work, and every single one of them is a Viking fan. I need some support from a fellow Packer fan."

"Sounds like fun," I said, trying not to jump up and down with excitement.

"Why don't you give me your email address and I will send you the information and directions."

We were by the fitness desk, so I found a pen and piece of paper to quickly jot it down.

I received an email shortly after I got to work. Two days later, I found myself driving thirty miles north to a party where I wouldn't know anyone. This was really stepping out of my comfort zone. I realized I wasn't going there for the game but to see Bryan.

His house was a one-level log cabin surrounded by woods. I was nervous going to the door. Was I making a mistake? But Bryan greeted me at the door and introduced me as a friend from back home. It didn't take long for the fear to melt away. His friends were welcoming, and before I knew it, they were already starting to banter with me about the game.

The party ended up being a blast even though the Packers lost. Bryan was a great host. I was made to feel comfortable in what I envisioned might be an uncomfortable situation. Bryan and I even had a chance to talk more than the quick chats we had at the gym. Time flew by, and it was time to say goodbye.

"Thanks for coming," he said.

"It was a lot of fun. Thanks for the invite. See you at the gym."

As I drove back home, I wondered if this could be the start of something. I hoped we could see each other more than just at the gym.

I am not sure how it started, but after the party, Bryan and I started talking on the phone, going out to dinner, going to movies, and just hanging out as friends. He was easy going and fun to be around. I knew I wanted to be more than friends, but I didn't know how he felt and was waiting for him to make the first move.

In early December, he asked me if I could pick him up from the airport. He had gone to Vegas for a long weekend with his friend. After I picked him up, we went to my townhouse to watch a movie.

"I got you something," he said as he handed me a small box. "It's just a little thank you for picking me up."

"You didn't have to get me anything," I told him while trying to play it cool. My heart was pounding.

Inside the box was a three-inch tall metal trinket box shaped like a Christmas tree. It had little ornaments adorning its branches with a gold star on top. When I flipped open the top, there was a hidden compartment.

"I know you aren't getting a Christmas tree this year, so I thought this would do. Everyone needs a Christmas tree."

"Bryan, thank you. This is so thoughtful. I love it."

"I'm glad you like it," he replied as he leaned in for our first kiss.

With the gift and kiss, I knew we weren't just friends anymore.

Shortly after we started dating, Bryan bought a house in Eagan about five miles from my townhome in Eagan, which made it very convenient to see each other on a regular basis. He had been looking at houses in the Eagan area before we started dating because he was tired of his thirty-mile commute to work in Burnsville from Blaine every day.

From the very start of our relationship, I knew how much biking was a part of Bryan's life. He had been bike racing since he was fourteen. Training didn't stop because it was winter. He would need to go ride his bike in the basement on most nights. He would either set up his bike on a trainer (a device to convert your bike into a stationary bike) or use his rollers (a device where you balance on top of metal drums while riding). Knowing that biking was so important to Bryan a few months after we started dating, I bought a bike of my own. Was it to impress him? Maybe. Most of our weekends in the spring/summer were dedicated to bike races. I even participated in my first thirty-mile bike race, which led to the start of training for triathlons. I knew that swimming was usually the hard part of triathlons, but I'd been a swimmer in high school, was a lifeguard, and had taught swim lessons, so that wasn't my issue. Now that I had a bike, I thought, why not?

Our relationship grew over the next two years. There was hardly a day when we weren't together. The talk of marriage came up, and we even looked at rings, but he would never totally commit.

It was Bryan's birthday in October of 2004, and we decided to take advantage of the perfect fall day—sunny, in the mid-sixties, with the leaves changing into breathtaking colors—and drove down to the Cannon Falls bike trail, which was about thirty miles from his house in Eagan. I had never been on the trail, which follows right along the Cannon River all the way to Red Wing, Minnesota. We had dinner reservations at 6:30 p.m. in Eden Prairie and needed to allow enough time to get home and clean up from our ride, so we decided to turn around at the fifteen-mile mark. We were about halfway back to where the car was parked when Bryan told me to pull off the trail. We happened to be by a Porta-Potty, so I asked, "Do you have to go to the bathroom?"

"No, just pull over."

"OK."

As I came to a stop, Bryan was fumbling with something on his bike.

"What are you doing?" I asked as Bryan started to get down on one knee. He held out the Christmas tree trinket he had gotten me when we started dating and opened it. There, sparkling inside the hidden compartment was an engagement ring—a plain white gold band that had a "floating" solitaire diamond at its center. Its brilliance took my breath away. I couldn't believe it! This was really happening. I don't remember what he said when he was on his knee, but I said "YES!" as he placed the ring on my finger. I was so excited Bryan could barely keep up with me as we made our way back to the car, my legs pedaling at super speed. I couldn't wait to call my parents and my sister. Unbeknownst to me, my parents had been waiting for the phone call because Bryan had called them earlier in the week to ask permission. They were beyond thrilled.

We were married six months later and made our home in Eagan, Minnesota. We had a picture-perfect life—two children, a nice home, good jobs—Bryan, a manager of MHC, a software company, and me, a kindergarten teacher. Along with our jobs, we played an active role coaching our kids' activities: hockey, football, lacrosse, and track.

The love of biking became an integral part of our family. We would go on family rides whenever we got the chance. The kids even started racing. At Bryan's bike races or my triathlons, there were always kids events they wanted to participate in. Griffin was even featured on the website for the Northfield Criterium bike race, racing at two-and-a-half years old with his training wheels. Two years later, Elyse followed in her big brother's footsteps.

We had it all. Our lives were going along flawlessly until today . . . *Would this be how our story ends? Our love story was like a romance novel and romance novels don't end like this. We need our fairytale ending. NO, NO, NO, it can't end this way.*

Chapter 6

I don't know how long I was standing there, staring at the doors that Bryan had been rushed through, when a hospital chaplain appeared and guided me to a bench. He sat with me so I wasn't alone. *What is happening? Is Bryan going to die? What am I going to do?*

Soon after I had sat down with the chaplain, a police officer came and sat with us. "Hi, I am Captain Jim Rogers. I work at the Dakota County Sheriff's Office."

"Hi," I said as I looked up to see a man in his early fifties with blond hair that was graying. He was in his uniform, a white shirt and brown pants.

"I'm sorry about your husband. We don't really know what happened except that Bryan was involved in a hit-and-run. Passersby stopped to get his bicycle out of the middle of the road. That's when they found Bryan lying in the grass."

"OK." No other words entered my brain. Blank. Shock had penetrated my whole body making thinking feel impossible.

Captain Jim broke the awkward silence. "It was a beautiful day for a ride. I went for a ride myself."

"Yes, Bryan was excited to be out riding. You couldn't have asked for a better day to go for a ride in March." *Why am I still talking about the weather?*

"We will do everything we can to find the person who did this. Here is my card. We will be in touch." He had a paper bag filled with all of Bryan's clothing, his helmet, and shoes. These items would be sent in for testing to see if there was any evidence transferred from the vehicle that hit him. He handed me Bryan's wedding ring, ear warmers, and wallet. "You can have these back."

"Thank you," I said as I slipped Bryan's ring onto my thumb and made myself a promise I would keep it on until Bryan could wear it again.

How could Bryan be hit and left for dead? How does a person just drive away from a human being? I imagined him just lying there. *Was he crying for help? Bleeding, broken bones, gasping for air?* It was too much for me to comprehend or imagine.

The chaplain helped me find Carmen and then led us up to the waiting area on the second floor. There was no one else there. It was a cozy area with a fireplace and soft chairs. A balcony overlooked a lobby area with a waterfall, grand piano, and chairs. It would be a nice place to sit, I thought, if I wasn't waiting for the doctor to tell me if Bryan was alive or not. Carmen and I didn't speak. We just sat in stunned silence, waiting. There was so much waiting. It was paralyzing and terrifying.

Bryan's dad, Steve, was on his way. I texted him to let him know where we were so he could find us once he arrived.

As Carmen and I sat there waiting, I tried to keep my body and mind busy so I didn't have to think about what was really going on. I made a mental checklist of people I needed to contact: my parents (✓), Bryan's parents (✓), Erica (✓), my coworker to get a substitute lined up for my class (✓). *Who else? Crap, I have to tell Bryan's work. I don't have any of his coworkers' phone numbers. Why would I? Wait, I am friends with his coworker Theresa on Facebook. I'll try to message her and let her know.*

I knew Theresa wasn't on Facebook often, but it was my only hope. I prayed she would get the message. I wrote, "Bryan was in a serious bike accident. Hit-and-run. He is in surgery now."

A few minutes later, Theresa messaged me back. "What? Shauna, can u call me? Here's my number."

What else can I tell her? I didn't know anything more than what I already had written. But I need to call her.

"Hi, Theresa. It's Shauna."

"Oh my God. What happened?"

"Bryan was involved in a hit-and-run on his way home. He is in surgery now. He won't be at work tomorrow."

"What hospital are you at?"

"North Memorial."

"OK. I will let others from work know. I'm so sorry."

"Thank you. I will be in touch."

Who else should know? Of course, I have to tell Steve. Steve was Bryan's college roommate and best friend, known to us as Stewy. By chance, I had his wife Tracy's number. I sent her the following text. "Hi, Tracy, this is Shauna Joas. Bryan has been in a serious bike accident. He was airlifted to the hospital and is in surgery now. He has a bad pelvic injury. That is all I know."

"Oh my gosh! Thank u for letting us know. Please keep us posted and let us know what we can do if anything. Prayers & Hang in there."

I can't do this individually, but I need to let others know. I will send the dreaded group text. I ran down my list of contacts, adding anyone whom I thought should know: Gregg and Shelly, Shani and Mike, hockey friends, etc. "Hi everyone. I want to let you all know that Bryan was in a serious bike accident on his way home from work. A hit-and-run. He is in surgery now. His pelvis is broken and he has internal bleeding."

Finally, Bryan's dad, Steve, arrived. He was a man who showed little emotion, but when I hugged him, we held each other in silence for a long time.

"He is in surgery," I said. "We're waiting for the doctor."

"OK."

"Where's Jan?"

"I couldn't get her to come. She has card club at our house tomorrow so was adamant on staying home. I told her, 'Bryan could die.' She said, 'Well, tell him I love him.' I had to leave her at home."

I couldn't imagine her not wanting to come be with her son but had to resist the urge to get angry. Jan had been diagnosed with dementia nine months earlier. She was the one who insisted on going to a neurologist. She knew something wasn't right. It wasn't just forgetfulness that comes with getting older. For a couple of years before the diagnosis, we had been noticing changes. She couldn't bring up the right words when having conversations. She didn't know what common things were called or know who people were. Her cognitive decline had gotten to the point where Bryan and I made the decision that we wouldn't let the kids go with her if she was driving.

Bryan and I didn't go to Chippewa Falls often to see our parents because we were so busy with the kids' activities, so I didn't realize Jan's illness had progressed this much. But she was clearly sicker than I thought. I was also shocked that Steve would leave her alone without getting someone to check in on her.

I noticed Carmen was texting with Jill to keep her updated. Back home, Jill let the kids watch a little TV. She knew she needed to stay calm and be matter-of-fact. She told me later that she kept telling the kids, "Your dad is strong. He's in good shape. We need to think positive."

Later, Jill told me that Griffin was so scared and sad, he thought Bryan was going to die. Jill asked Elyse a few times if she was OK. She continued to show no outward emotion. Griffin, who was our cuddler, asked Jill to lay with him as he fell asleep.

As we waited to hear from the doctor, my dear friend Catherine rounded the corner to the waiting room. She had heard the news from our colleague, Kristen. I ran to Catherine and hugged her. "Thank you for being here."

"I wouldn't be anywhere else," she said in her Irish accent. She was born in Ireland and lived there until she was in her twenties. I met her six years earlier when I was transferred to Red Pine Elementary. We both taught kindergarten and immediately connected. She had taken a year leave from teaching to go to Ireland with her daughter, Katie, who was training with an Irish swim team. She was supposed to still be in Ireland until July or August, but they had come back at the end of February because Catherine was getting displaced from Red Pine. She needed to interview for another position in our district. It was a tumultuous time for her with lots of unknowns, and yet, here she was. She somehow connected with my mom to ask if it would be OK if she went to the hospital. My mom said, "Go. I know she would want you there." I was so grateful she made the effort to come.

Dr. Farhat, the trauma doctor, finally came out around midnight. We had been waiting for about three or four hours. He was a tall man, with black spiky hair and sideburns. He seemed to be in his forties. "Bryan is in very critical condition," he said cautiously in a soft-spoken, gentle manner. Dr. Farhat was honest and factual with us as he continued. "He needed lots of blood and blood products. He's in the radiology area now. They need to put dye in him to find the source of the bleeding."

He's alive but still bleeding.

"Most of Bryan's trauma was in his pelvis. Once the radiologists determine the source, they will insert coils to try and stop the bleeding."

I never heard of what "coils" are, but they are going to stop the bleeding? I don't know how that is even possible.

Later, I Googled what Dr. Farhat was talking about with the coils. The medical term for this procedure is called coil embolization. The blood would form a clot around the coils, which would stop the bleeding.

"When he is stable enough, Bryan will be brought up to the trauma ICU floor. Our initial assessment is that he has a broken femur, broken pelvis, both hip sockets are broken, broken ribs, and broken lower back."

Ironically, a few days prior, Griffin had asked Bryan and me if we ever broke any bones. Bryan had been bragging to Griffin that he had never broken a bone in his life. I guess he spoke too soon. He was asking because my mom had fractured her shoulder at our house three days earlier when she fell down our basement stairs. After taking her to an orthopedic doctor first thing Monday morning, he recommended postponing their trip to Florida by a week. My mom declined and insisted they needed to go with plan B. The doctor put her arm in a sling to immobilize it and wrote a prescription for her to get a follow-up X-ray in two weeks to make sure her shoulder was healing correctly. My dad would have to do all the driving. Little did she know the prescription would be used in the Twin Cities, not in Florida.

"Bryan's broken bones will not be dealt with until Bryan is more stable," Dr. Farhat continued. My mind needed to focus on what Dr. Farhat was saying.

It seemed crazy that he would lie there with broken bones. *How long can he do that?* I was starting to grasp how dire the situation was. They wouldn't even bother with the broken bones until they knew Bryan wasn't going to die. *What is going to happen? How am I going to get through this?*

"Thank you," I said to the doctor.

"Someone will come get you and bring you up to the ICU waiting area."

Carmen had messaged our pastor to tell her what happened. Much later, Carmen would tell me, "I was ill equipped to help you. I didn't know what to say. I needed some guidance." Pastor Kris called her back an hour later and told her that she would be there soon. She told Carmen, "Just being by Shauna's side is enough."

We made our way up to the ICU family lounge. Again, there was no talking, just waiting. Around 1:30 a.m., the nurse came in to tell us we could go back and see Bryan. Just Steve and I went back. Catherine and Carmen stayed in the lounge believing it should be a private moment. Steve was silent as we walked side by side. I had never been so scared. *I wish my parents were here. I don't know if I am strong enough. What am I going to see?* My mind was telling me, *No, don't go back there,* but my body responded and followed the nurse. Nothing seemed real.

When we turned the corner, there was Bryan. He was surrounded by machines and IV poles. He had tubes coming out of everywhere, drains filled with blood and fluids that were leaking out of him, blood and medication being put back into him, nurses frantically moving about his room. The machines were keeping Bryan alive, but the beeping—oh the beeping. It was too much. Every time one of the alarms would go off, which seemed constant, I would panic and run out of the room covering my ears. I thought Bryan was dying. I couldn't bear it. It was like being trapped in a haunted house, scared shitless, knowing that something terrifying was about to happen. My heart was racing like I had just run the fastest one-hundred-yard dash of my life. I couldn't catch my breath. My fingers tingled, and my ears were hypersensitive, hearing every beep and chirp of all the machines.

Everything felt so out of my control, but I knew I had to keep going forward since that was the only way out. But I was petrified of what was coming around the corner. Every noise made me jump. I had to be ready for all that was happening. Every corner, a new terror. I knew it was going to be a long, long walk to get to the end of this. And what would the end look like? No matter how scared I was, I had to keep my feet moving forward.

Go back in. Bryan needs you. I would try to go into his room again. Luckily, Bryan had no trauma to his head or face. He still looked like Bryan, so I tried to just concentrate on his handsome face: scar over his left eyebrow from a previous bike crash, nose that was slightly pointed at the end, perfect ears with his little sideburns, widow's peak with his spiked up brown hair, slightly graying on the sides, thin lips and gapped teeth covered with a ventilator. There was a constant beeping, but when that beeping went faster or slower, alarms would start. And I would panic and run out of the room again, fear ripping through every part of my body. I didn't want to witness Bryan dying. The nurses weren't running into his room, so it must be OK? *Breathe. Get your heart rate back down.* I would build up my confidence and strength and then repeat.

Steve was very quiet. He stood next to Bryan and stared. There were really no words to say to each other. We weren't close enough to stand there hugging and comforting each other. I was never more terrified and lonely all at the same time.

After about an hour of going in and out of Bryan's room, my body, mind, and heart couldn't take it anymore. I was completely exhausted, as if hit by a truck. That would have a whole new meaning. Having been up for almost twenty-four hours, I staggered back to the lounge and collapsed on the loveseat around 2:30 a.m.

In the meantime, Bryan's coworkers, Theresa, Mike, and Jenny, were waiting in the family lounge. Pastor Kris arrived shortly thereafter. Every time Pastor Kris came, she would recite the same verse, "Even youths grow tired and weary, and young men stumble and fall; but those who hope in the Lord will renew their strength. They will soar on wings like eagles; they will run and not grow weary, they will walk and not be faint." Isaiah 40:30-31.

As a group, we stood in a circle, held hands, and prayed. Praying had always been uncomfortable for me. I never knew what to say. I grew up praying before dinner, "Come Lord Jesus, be our guest, and let these gifts to us be blessed. AMEN, Hallelujah." That was the extent of my prayers. So now, when I needed prayers the most, was God going to listen? I hoped and pleaded with all my might that God would.

Bryan had never been a "church guy." He didn't go to church growing up and told me from the start that, if I wanted our kids to grow up going to church, it would be my job. This didn't mean that Bryan wasn't spiritual. He'd always said, "My church is when I am biking."

I, on the other hand, grew up going to Central Lutheran Church in Chippewa Falls. When I moved to the Twin Cities, I searched for a church. After many, many visits to various churches in Burnsville, Apple Valley, Rosemount, and Eagan, I finally found a church that felt like home to me, Easter Lutheran Church by the Lake. I was genuinely welcomed as soon as I entered the doors. Easter by the Lake was more contemporary and reminded me so much of my church back home with more modern uplifting music led by the worship band. The pastors were relatable and didn't preach at you. Their sermons were inspirational and applicable to my everyday life.

The kids and I didn't go to church as often as I would have liked. I loved it when I went, but "things"—hockey, triathlon training, etc.—got in the way, but I didn't think God was keeping track of how many times I was there. I hoped not.

As we sat around the ICU family lounge, there wasn't a lot to talk about. Trying not to dwell on what was really happening, we engaged in small talk, keeping things light. Theresa and Mike were discussing how to "break into" Bryan's email. They needed to see if he had any meetings set up and contact the customers he was working with.

After another hour or so, everyone left except for Catherine, Steve, and me. Carmen had gone home to be with her kids and get them off to school the next morning. I went in to say good night to Bryan and told the nurses I would be in the family lounge if they needed me. I knew things with Bryan were bad. It was more than the normal bike crash, road rash and some broken bones. But was it so bad that he would die? I mean, they stopped the bleeding. Now, the doctors just needed to fix his pelvis and we could go home. Right?

The three of us each picked one of the leather loveseats to sleep on. The family lounge was divided into three parts with partial privacy walls. We picked the area on the left hand side, since there was already another family on the right side. There were family lockers on one wall, with a coffee maker and sink. A television hung in the corner. Big windows were over each loveseat. There were a few chairs and tables around the perimeter with a coffee table in front of the loveseats. I had no idea that this area would become my home away from home.

Chapter 7

Our friend, Shani, came around 5:00 a.m. the next morning. Shani being in the Twin Cities was another miracle put on our path. I had known her to be a caregiver to so many with her medical background and her deep faith. She was a fellow bicyclist's wife with the same fears that made us a tight-knit group, so when I saw Shani, I ran into her arms and broke down. It was the first time I really cried. It was a needed release of emotion that I didn't even realize I had been holding in. Shani and her husband, Mike, lived in Chippewa Falls. Mike was on the same bike racing team as Bryan. They had been on multiple cycling adventures over the past twenty years, with the last one being just two days before the accident. About a month prior, Shani had accepted a position as a professor of physical therapy at Concordia College in Saint Paul. She was living with a friend in the Twin Cities during the week and would go home to Chippewa Falls on the weekends.

Shani was a take-charge person with endless energy, exactly the type of person I needed. She got the report from the nurses to ground herself in the situation. I was in shock and on autopilot, not thinking clearly. I found myself counting on her to tell me what to do and guide me. "Talk to him, Shauna. He knows we are here. You can hold his hand. You aren't going to hurt him." Her guidance never stopped. She was someone we were able to count on throughout the whole ordeal.

Jill had stayed with Griffin and Elyse at night at our house to help keep the kids' environment as normal as possible. They were up late and didn't want to go to school. No one was going to argue with their reason. Catherine's seventeen-year-old daughter, Katie, volunteered to watch the kids the next day. Katie just returned from Ireland, so she was available to help as she was doing remote learning at the time. The accident news was likely not out, but having people asking about Bryan around school was something that neither kid wanted to deal with. Katie took the kids to Grand Slam, a venue with mini golf, bumper cars, laser tag, trampolines, and arcade . . . fun things to help distract them from what was happening to their world, but that was only the first day of an unknown period of time.

I called my parents early in the morning to update them. They were already in the car on their way back. Their long-planned month in Florida was no more. They had a thirteen-hour drive back to Wisconsin where they needed to switch out their summer clothes for early spring clothes (basically winter). Then they would continue the trek to our house in Minnesota to take over the care of Griffin and Elyse. I was so relieved and grateful to know they'd be here soon.

Mike, Shani's husband, arrived later that morning, as well as Gregg, another racing buddy from Superior, Wisconsin. Bryan, Mike, and Gregg had just met for a bike ride three days earlier in northern Wisconsin. Seeing Bryan lying there, being kept alive by machines, shook Mike and Gregg to their core.

"How could this have happened to Bryan?" Gregg asked. "He was the safest rider of all of us."

"It could have been any of us," Mike said, shaking his head. "We need to stay the course."

Bryan made it through the first night, but his numbers were off and he had no urine output. Dr. Beal was the trauma doctor working the day shift. He was an older doctor with brown hair and a bushy mustache. I could sense his tremendous knowledge and his devotion for his patients the first time he spoke with me. His gentle tone and demeanor were just what I needed.

"Bryan's body is acting like it's septic," he said, "but it seems too early. I would like to do surgery to look at his abdomen. That is where most of his trauma is located. I need to find out what's going on." I knew that this wasn't good but didn't understand the seriousness of sepsis.

Shani did, however. "Shauna," she said, looking directly into my eyes, "there is an infection somewhere in Bryan's body. Organs can begin to fail. Bryan needs this surgery."

I slowly nodded my head, starting to understand the gravity of the situation. But I didn't ask her if he was going to die. I thought if I said the word "die" out loud, then it would come true. I pushed that thought way back in my mind. "We will stay the course."

Dr. Beal needed to do surgery to check out Bryan's bladder because they hadn't really focused on that the night before. Since Bryan wasn't producing any urine, maybe the bladder or kidneys were damaged. Dr. Beal just felt like something wasn't right. I put all my trust in him. This man was truly an angel in our story. He had a gut feeling and it bothered him, so he acted on it. If he hadn't operated, I don't want to think about what could have happened.

The nurses were trying desperately to stabilize Bryan: checking his stats for his heart rate, blood pressure, oxygen, and adjusting the medications accordingly, measuring Bryan's output drains, hooking up the blood products and fluids he was receiving. As critical care nurses, they had to do a lot on their own. Since the doctor was not always there and they needed things stat, they needed to take the doctor's orders and adjust accordingly. They were professionals, just so cool and collected that I never had any real idea of how critical Bryan was. They just worked around all of us as we went in and out of Bryan's room.

I gave Bryan a kiss on his forehead. "I love you," I said. I left the room before the nurse unhooked the ventilator and connected the manual handbag resuscitator. I went to stand with everyone who was there by the elevators, saying well wishes and prayers as Bryan went into the elevator and down to surgery. This became the norm before each of Bryan's surgeries, his little cheering section of love and hope.

Dr. Beal came in after the three-hour surgery. He was shocked at finding a part of Bryan's large intestine septic and dying. Usually sepsis doesn't occur until twenty-four hours after a trauma, and it hadn't even been twelve hours. He removed that section of the large intestine. The bladder looked good, but the kidneys weren't working. The nephrologist, the kidney doctor, wasn't too concerned with Bryan's kidneys not working. It wasn't unusual with the trauma he sustained. He believed that the kidneys would just turn back on when they were ready.

That was crazy, something I never heard of, but I would again put my faith in the doctors that the kidneys would start working again when they were ready. The nurses continued to titrate the medications to try and stabilize him. Hopefully, getting out the septic intestines would help. But I was desperate to have him open his eyes and reassure me that he would be okay.

My sister, Erica, finally arrived from Chippewa Falls. I was lucky to have friends surrounding me, but there is nothing like family. My parents were in town, but they were keeping the kids away from the hospital, so it was so nice to have Erica be with me at the hospital. Just like everyone else, Erica has a busy schedule and responsibilities she needed to take care of before she made the trip. She had to get her third-grade classroom in order, sub plans written, and have things to get organized for her daughters before she could leave. My nieces were both in high school. Morgan was a junior and Ingrid was a freshman, so they could stay by themselves.

Growing up, Erica and I weren't close. We fought all the time. We hardly could be in the same room without it turning into a yelling match. I was the pesky little sister. Being four years younger was just enough of a difference that we were really at different stages in our adolescence. Who wouldn't look up to her? She was the popular cheerleader, dating the star basketball player, in the top five of her class. She had no time or patience for a little sister; I was invisible.

After Erica left for college, we became closer. But when Bryan and I began dating, that helped bring Erica and I even closer together. Bryan and Erica had been good friends all through school, elementary through high school. Luckily, they never dated each other, but they had gone on double dates together.

Right after Bryan and I got married, Erica got divorced from her high school sweetheart. This was when we really bonded. She needed someone to talk to and help her through the upheaval in her life. Now the tables were turned, and I needed her to be with me. I considered her my best friend and we talked on the phone at least three times a week. To have her with me during this dire, confusing, heart-stopping time was like having the comfort of your favorite stuffed animal.

Less than twenty-four hours after his accident, I knew I needed to start a CaringBridge site. My phone was constantly dinging. I realized people were just concerned about Bryan, but I couldn't keep up with all the text messages and emails. Things were changing second to second. CaringBridge was an easy way to communicate to everyone what was happening. And people we didn't even know could follow the story. We needed all the prayers we could get!

Stewy texted and told me he was flying up from Texas. He was scheduled to land at 1:00 a.m. on Wednesday morning. He had rented a car so didn't need anyone to pick him up from the airport. I waited up as long as I could, but exhaustion won and I fell asleep. Shani met Stewy in the hallway. They didn't want to wake me.

Bryan and Stewy had met in their freshman year at UW-Madison. They were both refereeing intramural soccer. They were on the same side of campus, so they would meet in the cafeteria. Both Bryan and Stewy had roommates they didn't get along with during their first semester. Stewy's roommate moved out, so Bryan moved in with Stewy. Thus began a lasting friendship.

We hadn't seen Stewy and his family in two years when we had stopped at their house in Dallas on our way to Galveston, Texas, for a spring break cruise. It was always such a good time when we were together, even if it was brief. We had even talked about taking a family trip together. Would we ever be able to do that?

When I woke up, Stewy was there. I jumped up and gave him a hug and thanked him for coming.

"I bought a one-way ticket," Stewy told me. "I'm not leaving until Bryan opens his eyes. I have to be with my buddy." Stewy's easy-going, laid-back attitude was shrouded with worry.

It touched my heart. I now knew what being a buddy really meant. If only Bryan knew Stewy was there.

Bryan was on three blood pressure medicines to keep his blood circulating and still getting blood or blood products every four hours or so. He was still in very critical condition. Dr. Beal wanted to take him in for surgery again because his numbers were showing that he was still septic. *Damn it. How can he still be septic?* Dr. Beal needed to find the source. Again I went in to say goodbye, kissed his forehead, and told him I loved him.

I had to leave again when they took him off the ventilator. My anxiety was at its peak when this happened. I knew the machine was breathing for him, and to see the nurse squeezing the bag to keep Bryan alive—it was just too much. One, two, three, four, five, squeeze. *What if they forget to squeeze?*

His life is literally in their hands. The sound of the air pushing out of the bag and going into his lungs reminded me of when Bryan would pump up his bike tires. This pre-surgery routing was becoming a norm. Taking a breath and putting my brave face on, I joined the cheering section at the elevators. It was a little bigger today.

While Bryan was in surgery, I went outside and had an interview with Reg Chapman, from WCCO News. It was my first of many interviews about the accident. Public speaking had always been one of my biggest fears, but compared to the nightmare I was living, this was a breeze. The one piece of advice Reg gave me was, "Set up a GoFundMe account. Your world has stopped, but the bills will keep coming. People want to help, and this is an easy way to allow them to."

My colleague, Kristen, had offered to set one up earlier, but I told her, "We are fine. We don't need any help. We have money saved." But after hearing Reg's advice, I called her and asked her to set up an account.

The police and county officers were desperately trying to find who hit Bryan. The reward money to find the driver was one thousand dollars. The road on which Bryan was hit was in a very rural area—not much traffic or many houses. Which was why he loved biking on it. The officers were going door to door asking questions, sitting at the intersection closest to the accident site to watch for a light-colored truck and following every lead that came in.

While in surgery, Dr. Beal had to remove the rest of Bryan's large intestine, most of his small intestine (leaving just enough to sustain life), and his gall bladder because everything was septic. *How is this even possible? How is Bryan going to live with the removal of almost all of his intestines? What will this mean for his quality of life?* But I couldn't let myself worry about that. Bryan was alive, so that was what we focused on, that was all I could do.

Dr. Beal was hopeful he got all of the infected area but couldn't see the lowest part of Bryan's rectal stump. The next morning, he scheduled a colonoscopy to see if the rectal stump was clear of sepsis. The levels in Bryan's blood were not good. With his kidneys not working, all the toxins weren't being filtered out of his blood. He was retaining so much fluid that the doctors needed to start dialysis. They would start with the slowest machine, which would take a full twenty-four hours to clean all of his blood. I had heard of people doing dialysis but never really understood the process. I learned that, as the machine takes blood out of the body, it cleans it from all the toxins and excess fluids, and then it puts the clean blood back in. It was crazy what they can do to help keep someone alive. Dialysis would help with Bryan's swelling by pulling off some of the extra fluid he was retaining. They were hoping Bryan's body could handle it.

After Bryan was hooked up to the dialysis machine, I asked nurse Kay if he was stable enough for me to go to Griffin's district hockey game. I hadn't seen the kids in two days, and I needed to make sure they were really okay. She told me yes, though looking back, I guarantee he wasn't. She knew I needed to go, since this was a big game for Griffin and would be good for the kids to see me. She had been with Bryan for most of his time in the ICU, and I felt confident in her. I knew she would take good care of him during the time I was away.

Erica drove me to Griffin's hockey game. She texted my parents to tell them we were coming. It was the first time in forty-eight hours that I had left the hospital. Shani, Mike, Steve, and Stewy were there and promised they would call me if anything happened. But I felt sick to my stomach. *What if Bryan dies while I am gone?* I would never forgive myself, but I needed to be there for Griffin too.

I was nervous as I walked into the arena. *What will I say? How will I react? How will everyone else react?* Luckily, the first people I saw were my parents. They were standing in the lobby waiting for me. They had just arrived in Minnesota earlier that day. I ran to them and suddenly couldn't contain my sobs, releasing all the fear and anxiety that I had been holding in.

My parents were my rocks. I'd relied on them my whole life. They were the first people I would call if I had a problem or needed guidance. Now I was in the biggest crisis of my life, and I needed them more than ever.

Their embrace was what I needed. I felt like a little girl engulfed by the protection of her parents. If only they could make things magically better like they did when I was little. This brief moment was exactly what I needed before I was surrounded by all the hockey parents.

As I walked into the rink, everywhere I looked, I saw the Snoopy Red Baron. A smile broke through the tears. It symbolized Bryan. He had a tattoo of the Snoopy Red Baron on his ankle. The rink was decorated with big posters of the Red Baron with the words "4 Coach Bryan." Stickers, with the same design, were on all the hockey parents, and each member of Griffin's team proudly wore the sticker on their helmets. It took my breath away, as goosebumps spread over my body. We were blessed with an amazing support system, not only for Bryan and me, but for Griffin and Elyse too.

When I walked into the stands to find a seat, I was shocked beyond belief to see our whole neighborhood there. Most of them had never been to a hockey game in their life. They were there to support Griffin and cheer him on. Even if only for a moment, in that cold hockey rink, the love of everyone wrapped me up like the comfort of a warm blanket. It felt so good. They embodied the words "Show up for people when they need it the most."

Elyse was running around with all the other sisters of Griffin's teammates. She said a quick hello and ran off, very much in Elyse fashion. I would have liked to have given her a hug and kiss, but she never let me do that before, so in a way I was glad she didn't let me now. It showed me that she was doing OK, at least that was what I told myself.

The game seemed like it was in slow motion, as if someone pushed the button on a DVD player. Usually I yell and cheer, but I just couldn't muster the strength. I sat like a zombie. The players, the puck, the cheering were going at a snail's pace. Each time one of the players scored a goal, they would skate over and tap the Snoopy poster. Even ten-year-olds understood the gravity of the situation. When Griffin scored a goal, the whole arena erupted in cheers. All I could do was sit and cry. So many emotions—*happy I am there, sad that Bryan isn't, wondering if he would ever be at a game again, scared of not being at the hospital, afraid my phone might ring, terrified of the future.*

The game went on and ended in a victory. They did it. They won for Bryan. This was the positive pick-me-up that Griffin needed. I knew he was sad and angry about Bryan.

As I walked out into the lobby, a parent from the other team came up to me. "I know you don't know me," she said, "but I am a friend of one of your friends. I wanted to let you know I'm sorry about your husband and am praying for all of you." I was struck by the realization that people knew who I was and knew what we were going through. This went beyond our inner circle of family and friends. I never imagined that our story would be one people were following, and now here we were. It made me feel connected and comforted.

Before I left the arena, everyone with tears in their eyes made sure to give me their hugs, love, and belief that Bryan would be OK, even the dads.

Then I needed to go. I wanted to go home and take a shower. I couldn't wait to wash away the hospital smell and just be alone with my thoughts.

Letting the hot water beat against my skin as the tears flowed was my release. I could have stayed there for hours, but the reality was that I had to go back. I dried off, dried my hair, and got dressed. As I walked by our bed, there was nothing more I wanted to do than crawl into it, pull the covers over my head, and wake up when this nightmare was all over. What would happen if I did that?

But that wasn't an option—for me, for Bryan, for the kids. I had to face that nightmare, which was now our life. I walked down the stairs. My kids, parents, and sister were waiting for me in the living room. It was time to go, the moment I dreaded . . . saying goodbye. Griffin and Elyse looked so small, scared, and confused. I can't even fathom what was going on in their heads. The kids and I had a group hug. I squeezed them for an extra-long time, with kisses on their heads. "I love you both so much, and Dad loves you, too," I said. "I will talk to you soon. Be good for Meme and Papa." Tears welled up in all of our eyes.

"We'll be good, Mom. We love you," they softly said with their heads down and tears rolling down their faces.

"Why don't you go to the front window to wave goodbye to Aunt Erica and me."

They walked to the window as I hugged and kissed my parents good-bye. "Love you. Thank you so much for coming back."

Then Erica and I were on our way, blowing kisses and waving, as we drove down the driveway.

I hadn't gotten any phone calls in the four hours since I'd been gone. I assumed no news meant things that stayed the same. Arriving at the hospital, the terror and anxiety settled once again in my chest. I nodded to Erica, put on a brave face, and walked back through the doors.

Chapter 8

Friday, March 11, 2016 (3 days after the accident)—the ultimate turning point and another day that will be etched in my mind and heart forever.

Early that morning, Bryan's bedside colonoscopy found that the top five centimeters of his rectal stump was non-viable. He was still septic. NO! *This is not the outcome I wanted to hear, based on what I recently learned from Shani about what being septic is. What would happen now?*

Bryan's numbers were very unstable. His heart rate and blood pressure were erratic. They had to give him medicine to get his heart back into rhythm, like an IED does. He was getting worse every minute. *Is this it? Is he going to die?*

Dr. Beal called a meeting and pulled me, along with Erica, Steve, Stewy, Mike, Shani, and Catherine into the family room. The family room was connected to the family lounge. It was a room that was always locked unless the doctor was meeting there with a family. I had seen families go in there a few times during our short time in the ICU. Most exited with somber expressions, knowing that the news they received was not what they prayed for. You never wanted to be brought to the family room

"We have the following options," Dr. Beal said, "One, we do comfort care."

Holy shit, comfort care? That means we will let him die as painlessly as possible! This was the first time I really understood the depth of Bryan's injuries. There was that word, DIE. The word I never wanted to hear or say. Now it was out and all the ramifications that came with it. I knew it was bad. He was on life support; he was having surgery after surgery, but they were going to fix him. They had to fix him.

"Two, do surgery. If there is any sepsis in what is remaining of his small intestine, I will close him up and we will put him in comfort care. Being that I removed all of Bryan's large intestine and most of his small intestine, he only has enough left to live. Your body needs your small intestine to absorb the nutrients you eat and drink."

My head was spinning. *What am I going to do? Am I going to be planning a funeral? Will Griffin and Elyse grow up without a dad? How could I do this alone?* Just when I thought things couldn't get worse than the two officers standing at the door three nights before telling me Bryan was in an accident, it did. After all of this, now I would have to decide if Bryan lives or dies. This can't really be happening.

"Three, do surgery. If the small intestine is clear of sepsis, then I will remove the part of the rectal stump that is septic and give him a fighting chance."

Stewy, being the voice of calm and reason, said, "OK, let me make sure I am understanding correctly. You do nothing and Bryan dies, OR you do surgery giving Bryan a chance at living?"

"That is correct," said Dr. Beal.

How has it come to this? I had to decide if Bryan lived or died. Bryan was going to die if Dr. Beal didn't do the surgery. There was only a miniscule chance that doing the surgery would save his life. There was a chance that

Bryan would not be strong enough to survive the surgery. I don't think he was really suffering with all the medication he was on, but Bryan's life was in my hands. There was really only one option—go for the surgery. If there was a chance of survival, however minimal, I had to take it.

"Do the surgery," I told him.

Dr. Beal immediately left the room. We were all in a state of shock, trying to comprehend what just happened. Then the tears started to flow. Mike said, "I think we need to pray." He led the prayer. I can't remember all that was said, but I do remember the words, "We need to stay the course." Then Catherine sent out the following message on CaringBridge: "We need a miracle."

> Journal entry by Shauna Joas—Mar 11, 2016
>
> Bryan is going in at 9:30 for surgery to try to save his life.
> The surgeon is checking to see first if his small intestine
> is still okay and if it is he is going to remove the 5 cm of
> rectum that is dead. If the small intestine is not viable,
> the surgeon will not proceed with the rest of the sur-
> gery and we will transition to comfort care. We need a
> miracle, so please everyone pray with all your might.

Erica called my parents and told them, "Brush your teeth and get here as fast as you can! It's not good."

My parents didn't want to scare the kids, so they told them, "We are going to bring breakfast up to your mom and aunt Erica. Katie is going to come and hang out with you again." They were excited Katie would be coming.

Carmen and her husband, John, drove my parents to the hospital. They were frantically trying to get there before the surgery. Of course, it was right during the morning commute, so this made it even more stressful for them getting there. This would be the first time my parents saw Bryan, which later my mom told me, "It was terrible seeing Bryan, but it was nothing like looking at the terror in your eyes, Shauna, nothing any mother should ever have to see."

It never crossed my mind to have the kids come and see Bryan. I didn't want their last memory of him to be the hospital room with all the tubes and machines coming off him. I could barely handle it. How could I expect an eight- and ten-year-old to do so? I couldn't traumatize them like that. If surgery didn't go the way we hoped, then I would bring the kids up to say goodbye. Was this right or wrong? I wasn't sure.

More people arrived at the hospital after receiving the CaringBridge update. They knew they needed to be there. Among them were some of Bryan's coworkers, my close friends, Jenny, Erik, and Angie, and Pastor Kris. Everyone went into Bryan's room, one by one, to wish him luck on his surgery. It took a couple of hours to get Bryan ready for surgery because he was so unstable.

For Bryan's previous surgeries, I had always left the room when they took him off life support and started bagging him. However, this time I knew I had to stay in his room with him. It could be the last time I saw him alive. Mike stayed with me. I was shaking so badly I was struggling to stand, my legs giving out again and again. Each time, Mike was there to hold me up.

It was hard for me to breathe with the fear crushing my chest. *How could this be happening? If this surgery doesn't work, Bryan is going to die. Even if it does work, there are no guarantees.* I held Bryan's limp, dead-looking hand, squeezing it and kissing it. "I love you, Bryan. You keep fighting. Griffin, Elyse, and I need you." I was trying to keep myself together.

I followed behind Bryan as they wheeled him to the elevator. Almost twenty people were standing in the hallway cheering Bryan on as he went into the elevator. The hallway was filled with a power and presence that we could all feel. It surrounded us. Whether the outcome would be the one we wanted, only God knew the answer. We would have to leave it in his hands.

When Bryan was wheeled through the doors, everyone dispersed into various areas of the waiting room. Now all we could do was wait and pray.

I still hear stories from people about how they stopped and prayed for a miracle when they received the CaringBridge update. The number of prayers that were being sent up for him was incomprehensible.

While everyone prayed Bryan would live, I prayed that I'd made the right decision. Yes, of course I wanted him to live, but I still didn't know if Bryan was paralyzed or had brain damage. Since he was on life support, there was no way to determine this. He was hit by a vehicle going at least fifty-five miles an hour, so I could only imagine the damage this did to his body and brain. Was this what he would have wanted? If he lived, what would his quality of life be? I prayed for him to send me a sign that I had made the right choice.

People were trying to get me to eat something. But it's impossible to eat when your stomach is up in your throat. I could hardly breathe. How was I going to eat? I appeased them by nibbling on a granola bar.

It might not have seemed like the appropriate time to be doing this, but Erica and I needed to get our spring break trips canceled. There was a time limit on getting our trips refunded. Erica had been planning to go to Florida where she and my nieces were supposed to stay with my parents. Shani was calling to cancel our spring break trip to Puerto Vallarta, which we'd just booked five days earlier.

I had been pressuring Bryan to book something. Spring break was a time when I needed to get away. As a teacher, it was a reset that got me through until the end of the school year. When we went on spring break, I could totally take a break. But Bryan was a procrastinator, always looked and waited for the best deal. I had had enough. Five days earlier, we'd gotten into a fight about getting something reserved. "Just book the trip!" I told him as I walked out the door to go to the store. An hour later, I got a text message, "It's booked. I have a bad feeling about this." I'm not sure if he said this because it was the first time we were taking the kids to Mexico or because he felt rushed into making a decision. Now his words felt prophetic.

Bryan's dad had stayed at the hospital since he drove up the night of the accident. Later I'd learn that he told my dad that he couldn't leave the hospital because he had to make sure I was making the right decisions. "After all, I am his dad," he'd said. I'm glad I didn't know about this conversation until a few months later. *What does he mean? Does he think I am not handling the whole situation correctly and has to be there to step in?* When I learned this, it felt like a slap in the face.

Because Steve was there at the hospital, it meant Jan had been home by herself, which wasn't safe for her. So it was arranged that Jan would take a shuttle bus from the airport in Eau Claire, Wisconsin, to the Twin Cities airport. A friend of hers made sure she got on the shuttle bus that morning. As we were sitting around waiting while Bryan was in his life-or-death surgery, Steve jokingly said, "I hope she gets off at the right place."

You could hear a pin drop.

"I guess I shouldn't have said that," he said quietly.

My mom replied, "No, you shouldn't have."

Steve made Jan's shuttle reservation to have her exit at Terminal 2. This airport is the smaller of the two Minneapolis–Saint Paul airports. With only fourteen gates, there isn't too much going on. He thought it would be easier for someone to pick her up there. Unfortunately, since the shuttle stopped at Terminal 1 first, that was where Jan got off. Terminal 1 has one hundred seventeen gates—a massive airport with a high volume of travelers and non-stop traffic. It makes it overwhelming and confusing for anyone, let alone someone with dementia.

Carmen and John had offered to pick up Jan so Steve didn't have to leave during this critical time. He gave them the details of when and where she would arrive. When it was past the time of arrival, Carmen decided to go into the airport, to see if Jan somehow ended up in there. There was no sign of her, so Carmen called Catherine, "We can't find Jan. Can you have Steve call her to find out where she is?"

When he called, she didn't know where she was.

"Well, she is not at Terminal 2," Carmen said. "I've looked all over. We'll head over to Terminal 1. It's only a mile away. Keep Jan on the phone so we know where to pick her up."

Catherine rolled her eyes and then whispered to Steve, "Step out into the hallway. Shauna does NOT need this added stress right now of this three-way conversation!"

I tried to block out the muffled conversations happening in the hall and just concentrate on breathing and praying. Bryan was my main concern.

Jan couldn't tell Steve the color of her jacket or articulate any visual descriptions of what was around her. Steve finally convinced Jan to ask someone where she was. The person told her she was in the check-in area. She must have followed the other shuttle passengers off the bus, across the street, and into the airport. Steve told her, "Find a bench and sit down. Stay there and don't leave. Carmen and John are coming to pick you up."

John dropped Carmen off so she could go in and find Jan. Since you can't stop for an extended period of time in the drop-off zone, John looped around until Carmen called to tell him she'd found Jan. When Carmen found Jan, she told her that she was there to pick her up. Jan was a bit tentative but was at the point in her dementia where she was oblivious to any safety concerns and went with Carmen. It was more of a scary and disorienting experience for us than it was for Jan. I was annoyed—I didn't want any of the positive energy in the room distracted from where it should be going—to Bryan.

The surgery took longer and longer. We contemplated whether that meant good news or bad news. In my head, I decided good, right? Gregg and his wife, Shelly, arrived from Superior. They had come as soon as they could. It was almost a three-hour drive. We ran to each other and embraced. There was a silent understanding being fellow cyclists—this could have been any of us, and we would be there for each other.

After almost four hours, the nurse came around the corner. My heart sank. *What is she going to say?*

"Bryan is out of surgery. Dr. Beal will meet you in the family room. He wants to talk to you."

He made it through surgery. He made it through surgery! But what did Dr. Beal find? What will Dr. Beal say? Will it be good or bad?

We all couldn't fit in the room, so some had to stay outside. I remember feeling terrible about this; everyone there was "family," so how could I pick who came in the room and who didn't? I decided I would go in the room and the others would have to figure it out themselves.

We all just quietly sat and stared at each other. It seemed like another eternity for Dr. Beal to come into the room. My heart was racing. I was so scared. *Do I really want to hear what Dr. Beal is going to say? This could be a life changing moment. Am I ready?*

Finally, he came in, closed the door, pulled a chair so he was right in front of me, sat down, and looked directly into my eyes. With tears in his eyes he said, "We got our miracle, Shauna. Surgery went well."

While everyone cheered, yelled, hugged, and cried, I put my hands over my eyes and wept. I finally got to exhale. Dr. Beal patiently waited while we quieted down and then proceeded to tell us, "The small intestine looked good. I removed eight centimeters from the top of the rectal stump. Now we just wait and see how Bryan responds. It will be a long road, but I am more optimistic now."

I gave him a huge hug. "Thank you, Dr. Beal. Thank you."

"I'm just doing my job," he answered as he quietly slipped out the door.

We opened the door to the family and shared the news with the others waiting outside. The tears that were so sad and hopeless before were now tears of exuberance and optimism. Everyone was hugging each other, jumping up and down, giving each other high fives. You would think that we had just won the Tour de France. But finally, we had something to celebrate.

As we were leaving the family room, Carmen and John arrived with Jan. She looked disheveled. Her gray hair stood up like she had stuck her finger in a light socket. She had an absent look in her eyes with a constant grin that reminded me of the Cheshire cat from *Alice in Wonderland*. There was no concern for Bryan. She only wanted something to eat because she was hungry. She found the snacks that were laid out and helped herself. I resisted the urge to be angry at her. The dementia was more advanced than we realized. And anyway, I'd just gotten my miracle.

Once everything settled down, late in the afternoon, my parents and Bryan's parents took off for our house. My mom called when they arrived home. "You aren't going to believe this, but your neighbors, Jill, Patrizia, and Melissa, came and cleaned your house from top to bottom. Jill wanted to ask if it was OK, but Melissa said, 'We aren't going to ask; we're just going to do it.' They also did all of the laundry; whether it was dirty or not, it got washed. Shauna, you have the best friends."

My eyes filled with tears again. "I never in a million years would have asked someone to clean my house and do the laundry, but man, what an awesome thing to do. Now you and dad don't have to worry about that for a while."

"Call if anything comes up," my mom said. "Otherwise, we will talk to you tomorrow. I love you."

"I love you too, Mom."

By that evening, Bryan had been taken off of two of the blood pressure medicines. His heart rate and blood pressure were equaling out. Bryan was showing me the answer . . . *I did make the right decision.*

Chapter 9

As I woke up the morning after the miracle surgery, I looked out the window of my makeshift bedroom, in the family ICU, to the most breathtaking sunrise. The gray cloud that had been hanging over us was being washed away by the sun. The reds, oranges, and purples seemed to wrap around me and gave me hope and peace that things were going to be OK. It was a new day. The worst was behind us.

I grabbed my phone to capture this magical splendor when it beeped. It was a message from Chaz, my good friend Angie's husband. "I don't even think Bryan knows how much of a fighter he is. The sunrise is beautiful right now. It's going to be a good day, Shauna."

Yes, indeed it was. I knew I still had to walk down that hallway to Bryan's room, not knowing what I would see, but the sunrise gave me a new-found strength to handle what was to come.

I took a deep breath and went to see him. There he was, lying there still surrounded by the machines keeping him alive, the beeping with every fluctuation in blood pressure, heart rate, or oxygen levels, the swishing sound of the air being pushed into his lungs and then sucked back out, the suction from the wound VACs pulling out blood and fluids, and the dripping of the

IVs. The sounds alone still made me want to turn and run, but today was a new day.

Bryan's beautiful green eyes were slightly open and bulging out with an absent stare—not how Bryan ever would have looked—so I put a washcloth over them. I noticed that he also had clamped down on his tongue, which was sticking out around the ventilator. It looked as if he had almost bitten his tongue in half. His body was so swollen. It looked as if his skin might rip at any moment. He was still hooked up to so many machines and tubes.

The nurses had put braces on Bryan's feet that kept them at a ninety degree angle to keep his calves stretched to prevent foot drop. There was a special mat under Bryan, with handles, that allowed the nurses to slide Bryan on the bed. A big concern was bed sores for a person who was immobile, so they didn't want him lying in the same position for too long. He needed to be rolled side to side. Could there be any more medical devices attached to him? But, I reminded myself, this was all going to move us forward. I reached for Bryan's hand, which was cool, and gave it a squeeze. "You're going to make it," I whispered.

The doctors decided to give Bryan one day of rest between surgeries or procedures. Tomorrow, Bryan would have surgery to make a stoma, which was where Bryan's waste would come out. But today his body needed a break. Four surgeries in the first four days was hard on a body, let alone a body that was not fully functioning.

Later that day, Bryan's older sister, Gina, arrived from Alabama. I was shocked she even came, being that there wasn't a strong bond between them. Even growing up, they weren't close. We only heard about Gina and her family through Jan. There was no direct communication between Bryan and Gina, and there hadn't been for twenty years. Gina and I never really connected, either. There was no initiative from either Bryan or Gina to interact. Now with Jan's dementia, the relationship was even more severed. Maybe, just maybe, Bryan's accident was what would bring the two of them closer together, and maybe Gina and I would also develop a relationship. I was cautiously optimistic. We greeted each other with an uncomfortable obligatory hug.

"Thanks for coming."

"Of course."

I found we didn't have a lot to talk about besides surface conversation for a short time. Gina, Jan, and Steve went back to see Bryan. I stayed in the family lounge because I felt they needed their private time with him. They weren't gone long.

"I think we are going to head to your house and get Gina settled," Steve told me.

"We will see you in the morning," Gina said and waved goodbye.

"OK, sounds good," I replied.

It was a long but uneventful day, which was a welcome relief after the last four days. I was ready to lie down and try to get a good night's sleep. Tomorrow will be another surgery day.

Chapter 10

At this point, the end of Bryan's intestine was sewn shut but still in his abdomen. This was a temporary fix only lasting a couple of days before the waste would start leaking. If that happened, it could be deadly—hence, the stoma. The doctors explained that Bryan's stoma would be located on the right side of his abdomen, below his ribs. They would take the end of his intestine and fold it inside out, like when you cuff the bottom of your pants. He would have an ileostomy bag for his intestinal waste, aka poop. The hope was that, after Bryan recovered, the doctors would be able to reconnect his organs so his human plumbing would be as close to normal as possible. The main issue was fluid absorption within the digestive tract which was one of the primary functions of the large intestine, that he no longer had. Therefore, it was much more likely when Bryan got through all the medical procedures and his body physically recovered and adapted, he still would need to keep the ileostomy for the rest of his life. This was currently a small issue that would not need to be addressed for months down the road.

I was with Bryan while they were preparing him for his fifth surgery. They were running late, so I was in his room longer than usual. After they took him down to surgery, I went back to the family lounge to wait. I noticed that Jan, Steve, and Gina were gone.

"Where are Jan, Steve and Gina?" I asked Stewy and Catherine.

"Jan was having such intense abdominal pain that they took her down to the emergency room," Catherine answered.

"Seriously, what else could happen?"

They were gone for a long time. Stewy said, "Shauna, Catherine and I will go and check on them and find out what's going on."

When Catherine and Stewy got back, Catherine said, "It was very crowded in the ER. She finally got into a room. They were going to run a bunch of tests, but they suspect it is a bladder or kidney infection."

Stewy said, "There is also a funny story we have to tell you about something that happened in the ER waiting room."

The nurse stepped into the lounge to tell us that Bryan was back from his surgery. "You can go back and see him."

"We'll tell you the story later," Stewy continued.

We went back to see Bryan. The surgery had gone well. Bryan's abdominal wound was still oozing at a slow but constant rate, which was normal and not worrisome. His abdomen remained open about six inches. It had remained open since the first abdominal surgery. It was covered by a wound vac, which is a vacuum drain that pumps out excess fluid and air from his wound. Since the body heals from the inside out, they needed to be able to monitor that it was healing and there were no new infections. They would start the process of closing his abdomen muscles in a few days. It would take a few surgeries to do this, slowly stretching the skin and muscles together again a little at a time.

He had significant bleeding at the stoma site. So much so, it required him to have another blood transfusion. I never realized how much blood was needed for one trauma patient. So far, Bryan alone had needed twenty units of blood, twenty units of plasma, seven units of platelets, and three units of cryoprecipitate.

If people hadn't donated blood, Bryan wouldn't be alive. That is why we say, "One donation can save three people's lives." Why wouldn't you want to do that? It's ironic that it was Bryan who initially encouraged me to donate blood. Very early on in our relationship, we donated blood as a "date night." Now being on the receiving side, I am in awe of how that simple act truly gives people life.

Gina popped her head in the room and said, "My dad and I are taking my mom to your house. She has a severe bladder infection. She is going to take the prescribed medication and rest. We'll be back later."

"OK. I am glad it wasn't anything too serious," I said. *I don't think I could have handled any more on my plate, and yet, my concern was that, with only one car, taking Jan back to Chippewa wasn't an option. I was frustrated that they would be leaving Jan at our house for my mom to care for. Would Jan be able to take her medication at the right times, or would my mom have to do that too? My mom is still in a sling with her broken shoulder and really didn't need to be worrying about Jan, along with taking care of the kids. But according to Steve, "Jan's fine."*

Later that night, when we were hanging out in "our room," Catherine said, "It's time for a good laugh. Stewy, tell the ER story."

Stewy chuckled and shook his head. "This is a classic. I sat down next to Jan in the ER, and she kept staring at my head, moving her head back and forth, as if trying to solve a problem. I knew she was looking at my receding hairline."

"What?" I said giggling.

"Finally, Jan asked, 'Do you shave your head like that on purpose?'"

Stewy smirked and paused. "'No,' I said as seriously as I could, 'this is the path God chose for me.'"

We all burst out laughing.

Stewy held up his hand. "Wait there's more. Jan nodded and said, 'Well, you have a very nice head.'"

Our laughter got even louder.

Dementia is a serious issue that impacts a large percentage of people as they age, but it was nice to have a moment of laughter to break the otherwise somber atmosphere, even if it was an insensitive reaction.

Before going to bed, I went to say good night to Bryan, and I noticed that he had some bruising around his eyes. It was yellowish, like when a bruise is fading and almost gone. Then over the next few days, the yellow slowly started to spread across the rest of his body. This wasn't bruising but jaundice. The doctors didn't seem too worried. They told me it was very typical when there was trauma to the liver. I hadn't realized or been told he'd had trauma to his liver, but the list of medical issues we had to get through would continue to get longer throughout his hospital stay.

What I learned on this day was that, when a person has liver issues, the bilirubin numbers in their blood would increase until they hit a plateau and then they would go back down. The higher levels of bilirubin in Bryan's blood caused him to become jaundice. The doctors would continue to monitor Bryan's numbers and watch for the plateau. Every day he was getting more yellow. Even the whites of his eyes were yellow. With all of his swelling and being yellow, he looked like a glowing yellow Oompa-Loompa from the *Charlie and the Chocolate Factory* movie. I even asked if they could use the same light on Bryan that they use for babies with jaundice. The doctor looked at me and smiled, "That won't work for Bryan."

Monday was another day of rest for Bryan, meaning no surgery. Bryan already had five surgeries in six days, with many more to come. This was a welcome relief for Bryan's body, as well as my mental stability. Since it would be a quiet day, we decided Gina and Steve would stay at the hospital, and Stewy and Shelly would take me home so I could shower.

After seven days of intense stress and anxiety, leaving the hospital felt like coming out of a dark cave. It was dizzying getting in the car and going home. My brain couldn't focus on doing something normal. Everything we drove by—stores and other people in cars—it all seemed surreal.

When I got home, I went right upstairs to take a shower. The kids had gone back to school, so they weren't at the house. I was happy they were getting back into their normal routine but sad not to see them. I was so looking forward to the hot water pounding down on me and just having some time to myself. But right as I was about to step into the shower, my phone started ringing. My heart started racing. Did something happen to Bryan?

When I answered, it was the doctor calling me to get my permission to have Bryan taken down for a new dialysis port, feeding tube, and pelvic X-rays. I had always been at the hospital to sign the paperwork any time Bryan needed a surgery. Seriously, they didn't know they were going to be doing this before I left? I had hardly left Bryan's side, and now I wasn't going to be there for one of his procedures. I know it was only a few procedures, but damn it, I felt so guilty not being there. Would Gina and Steve go to wish him luck? I wasn't even sure they would notice Bryan was gone.

I showered quickly, likely not even washing all the soap from my body. Then I shoveled in some food, and Shelly and Stewy rushed me back to the hospital. It was definitely not the relaxing reprieve I had hoped for and desperately needed.

When we got back, Bryan was just being wheeled back to his room. Everything had gone well. Now that the feeding tube was finally inserted into his stomach, they could finally start getting Bryan some nutrition. With all the trauma to Bryan's gastrointestinal system and removal of so much of his intestines, fingers were crossed that his stomach was ready for the feedings. They would start very slowly at twenty milliliters per hour.

Unfortunately, after just a few hours, Bryan threw up and feedings were stopped. I wondered how Bryan could throw up when he was still on life support and in a coma. But he did. Everything they were putting into him came up and out of his mouth around the ventilator.

When we were hanging out before bed, Stewy's wife texted, "You got an ass." They had been talking about getting a donkey for their hobby farm, and she had bought one. This would be an ongoing joke to help lighten the mood. "You have a nice ass." "Your ass is cute." Stewy had been taking the night shifts sitting with Bryan. I am sure Bryan heard an earful from Stewy about his new donkey.

Since Bryan's kidneys were still on hiatus, dialysis was now a daily or an every-other-day process. "The kidneys are a very sensitive organ. When the body experiences trauma, the kidneys can just shut off. This can last from a few days to many weeks, even months," the nephrologist told us.

Because Bryan was somewhat more stable, he was able to tolerate the four-hour dialysis process now versus the twenty-four-hour one. It is the same process but at a much faster rate. There had to be a special nurse with Bryan at all times when he was doing dialysis to closely monitor his heart, oxygen, and blood levels. Those levels could plummet at a moment's notice. During every dialysis cycle, they were able to remove three to six pounds of fluid. Removing the fluid would help when the doctors begin the process of closing Bryan's abdomen. His abdomen was so swollen it was already stretched to its limits. So with some of the fluid removed, the skin would have more elasticity.

Every weekday on the trauma floor, between 10:00 a.m. and 11:00 a.m., the trauma doctors, pharmacists, therapists, and anyone else involved in the patient's care went from room to room discussing each patient. They reviewed what had happened and discussed what was next in the care plan. Since Bryan had been in surgeries every weekday since he arrived at the hospital, there had never been a meeting for him. Today was another surgery day—they would begin closing Bryan's abdomen—but that wasn't scheduled until the afternoon, so this would be our first time seeing the doctors during their rounds.

When Erica, who was going to spend the day with me at the hospital, arrived that morning, she came to the lounge to find me. "Did they move Bryan's room, because he isn't there?"

"No," I told her in a panic. I had been just about to head back to wait for the doctors to round, and now my heart was racing as I ran to Bryan's room. He wasn't there. What the hell was going on? "Where is he?" I yelled to the nurses. I hate being disrespectful, but I was hysterical.

"We took Bryan down early for surgery," a nurse said.

"What? Why didn't anyone tell me?" I said.

"I am so sorry," she apologized, putting her hand on her chest. "I think there was a miscommunication. Someone was supposed to tell you."

My body was trembling, first from panic of Bryan being lost to now furious they took him to surgery without telling me. They knew I was there twenty-four seven. I was trying to hold back tears of rage mixed with sadness. How could they do this?

No one had been at the elevator to wish him luck as we had for every other surgery. It was a ritual, something I needed. *What if something happens in surgery now because we didn't wish Bryan luck and cheer him on?*

I was doubly sad because Stewy was leaving today at 11:00 a.m. and was planning to spend time with Bryan, saying goodbye and having his daily "guy talk" with him. But now Bryan was already in surgery.

When Stewy arrived, I could see the hurt and disappointment in his eyes. I knew he felt conflicted about leaving. When he arrived seven days earlier, on his one-way ticket, he said he was staying until Bryan woke up. Unfortunately, that didn't happen. But he had to get back to his job and family.

I didn't want Stewy to leave. He was such a calming presence. He was quiet with a quick wit. I could see why Bryan had chosen him for a friend.

The kid in me wanted to grab his leg and not let him leave, but the adult in me gave him a hug and said, "Until next time."

Steve, Jan, and Gina came to the hospital to say goodbye to Bryan before they took Gina to the airport. Jan had the patience of a toddler so couldn't sit for very long. She would get up and start wandering down the halls.

"Where is she going?" I asked Steve.

"She's fine," Steve replied, making no attempt to get up and follow her.

She could get lost and end up, well, who knew where? After a minute or two, I went and looked for her. Jan had already made it back to Bryan's room. She was shaking him, trying to wake him up and pulling at his tubes. The nurse that was in the room looked at me and empathically said, "She is not allowed back here by herself."

"I'm so sorry," I said, both embarrassed and infuriated. "She has dementia. I'll make sure this doesn't happen again." Jan seemed confused as I guided her back to the lounge. She sat down and immediately pulled out her iPad to play Solitaire.

"I found Jan in Bryan's room trying to wake him up. She was pulling at his tubes. The nurse told me that she is not allowed to go to the room by herself."

"OK," Steve answered. Jan was oblivious to the conversion we were having.

OK? That's it? I couldn't even look at him, I was so angry. I had enough on my plate right now and couldn't handle "babysitting" Jan.

Over the few days Gina was at the hospital, we didn't connect as I'd hoped, but we did have a conversation about the fact that Steve was still letting Jan drive around Chippewa Falls on her own. It was infuriating yet scary that she was behind the wheel of a car when she clearly was not capable. Bryan and I had talked to Steve, seven months prior to the accident, about putting an end to Jan driving, but he didn't listen to us. I thought maybe he would listen to his daughter if she voiced the same concerns. I asked her directly if she would talk to her dad about this matter. Gina agreed, but whether or not she talked to Steve, I didn't know. After the way Jan behaved in Bryan's room, it was clear that she was not making safe choices, and not only had she lost memories, she also lost knowledge—driving was too risky.

It was time for them to leave because Gina needed to get to the airport. We said our goodbyes. As the three of them walked down the hall, I wondered when I would hear from Gina again.

It was a relief to learn that Bryan's abdominal surgery went well. Dr. Farhat was able to close his abdomen one inch on each side. This doesn't seem like a lot, but Bryan's abdomen was still so distended, the skin and muscles could only be stretched a little at a time.

I was exhausted by the end of the day. The highs and lows left me drained. Thank goodness Erica was there to sit with me the rest of the day. I could feel the exhaustion taking hold of me. I couldn't keep my eyes open any longer and felt myself falling asleep with Erica promising to stay on guard.

Chapter 11

Mornings were the worst. The anxiety in my chest and the overwhelming fear would consume me as soon as I opened my eyes. Even with the constant dread, I couldn't cry. My body wouldn't let me. Maybe it knew that, if I started, I wouldn't stop. There wasn't time for it. But making myself walk down the hall to Bryan's room was torture. I was back in a haunted house and the nightmare was beginning again, so what bad news would jump out and scare me today?

But once I was in his room, I settled into what had become our routine. It was as if the lights would come on and the scary shadows would go back into hiding. I would kiss his forehead and say, "Good morning." I would have a short one-way conversation with him while I massaged his dry arms and feet with lotion. When people are in a coma, no one really knows what they can hear and feel. I hoped that talking with Bryan and physically touching his extremities helped keep his brain and body connected. It also made me feel like I was actively contributing to his healing process.

After massaging and talking to him, I would go down to the cafeteria and have a quick breakfast by myself. North Memorial made the best bacon. I would sit at one of the cafeteria tables and watch as doctors and nurses and,

I assumed, family members of patients came and went. No one knew each other's stories, but no matter what, we did have a unique bond of being at the hospital living in the moment, whether it was good or bad.

Then, I would get ready for my day. I started with a daily sponge bath in the family lounge's bathroom sink, brushed my teeth, changed my underwear, and put on a new set of twenty-four-hour attire. I would head back to Bryan's room to wait for the update meeting with his medical team, which would be followed by a break in the lounge to recharge.

I was hardly ever alone during the day or evening. My parents would come to the hospital at least every other day after they dropped the kids off at school. They came to keep me company and bring things I needed: clean clothes, the mail, water, and snacks. It was so nice reading all the cards that people were sending. Their encouraging words refilled my depleted bucket. I kept track of all the cards, gift cards, and donations, knowing that I would write "thank-yous" to each and every one.

So many people—friends, friends I hadn't spoken to in years, neighbors, parents of students, and acquaintances—took time out of their lives to bring lunch, dinner, treats, or just sit with me. I can't tell you what a blessing that was. Like Carmen told me, "People will just show up. They may not know what to say, but they are there." That held true for us. People showed up over and over again, and they never expected anything in return. It helped take my mind off of the situation, even if it was only for a few minutes at a time.

Occasionally I felt jealous, though. I hate to admit that, but I did. Friends would come and bring me a meal, sit with me for a while, and then they would get to leave. They would get to go back to their lives—work, kids' activities, watching TV, and sleeping in their own bed—while I sat here, trapped in the Haunted House, my life in a holding pattern. I couldn't bring myself to leave the hospital, but even if I went home, my life was still in utter chaos.

I continued to sleep in the ICU waiting room every night, along with at least one other friend. My friends set up a schedule so that I would never be alone at night. From the beginning, our friends Shani and Mike, Shelly and Gregg, made a commitment to be there for however long we needed them. They promised they would stay the course with us.

Shani stayed every week night, and Shelly and Gregg drove down from Superior, Wisconsin, to stay every weekend. Mike came from Chippewa Falls at least once a week. They would go and check on Bryan during the night to allow me to get a good night's sleep.

Shani was a doctor of science in physical therapy. Every night she would come to the hospital after teaching all day at Concordia University in Saint Paul, Minnesota. She would then work on Bryan, moving and stretching his arms, legs, hands, and feet. She taught me things I could do during the day while she was gone. Keeping Bryan flexible and his muscles stretched were key to helping in his recovery. It allowed his joints to be more mobile and keep his muscles lengthened so that, when he did have the ability to sit upright or bear weight, we wouldn't run into muscle contractures and joint limitations.

Shelly was a RN. She was my medical interpreter and helped explain to me what all the numbers on Bryan's monitors were. This was what I needed so I didn't have to run out of Bryan's room every time an alarm would go off. She was able to clarify all the medical stuff that I didn't understand in layman's terms.

Both Shani and Shelly kept me focused on the immediate situation and what I could control. They wouldn't let me start dwelling on what the future might be. "You guys, what if Bryan is paralyzed? Our whole lives would change. We will have to sell our house, our car—"

"Shauna, stop right there," Shelly said.

"Do NOT go there," Shani said. "If, and I mean IF, that is the outcome, we will deal with it then."

"Focus on what is right in front of us at the moment," Shelly continued. "We got you!" Shelly and Shani surrounded me in a group hug.

I would listen to their advice. There was so much unknown at this point that I couldn't waste my energy on worrying about it.

I had known that Shani, Shelly, and I were friends. But I'd always felt like Bryan and I were the third wheel in the friendship group. Mike and Gregg had been friends since college. They had lived together for seven years. Then it was the four of them. Bryan and I became a part of the group when Gregg started racing for Spring Street Sports, based out of Chippewa Falls. That was the team Bryan had been racing for since he was in high school. Mike, Gregg, and Bryan connected, even though Mike lived in Chippewa Falls and Gregg in Superior. They would meet up to ride on the weekends when they weren't racing. The bonus was that Shani, Shelly, and I got along so well, too. Shelly and Gregg's son and Mike and Shani's nephew are all around the same age. It was a perfect fit.

Shani and Shelly showed me that Bryan and I weren't the third wheel in our group; we were family. They stopped their lives to support us. They never wavered on their promise to us.

I needed them and I needed everyone else who stepped up to help us, because even though Bryan had survived the miracle surgery, he was still in critical condition and things were still changing at a moment's notice. North Memorial is twenty-five miles away from our house and on the exact opposite side of the Twin Cities. Traffic and major construction made the drive at least forty-five minutes one way. Bryan's condition was still so critical, I didn't feel like I could leave. In my head, I thought that when Bryan "woke up," it would be like the movies. He would just wake up and start talking to me. So I wanted to be there. I wanted to be the first face he saw. I didn't want him to be scared or to panic. I wanted to be the one to explain that he was in an accident and in the hospital.

Every night was the same: I would call home to touch base with the kids.

"Hi, Griff."

"Hi, Mom."

"How was your day?"

"Good. How's Dad doing?"

"Dad is doing good. He is fighting to get better."

"OK."

"Be good for Meme and Papa."

"I know."

"I love you."

"Love you, too."

"Can I talk to Elyse?"

"OK."

Then I would repeat a very similar conversation with Elyse. The conversations varied slightly depending on their after-school activities.

After talking with both kids, I would talk to one of my parents to get an update, whether it be about schoolwork, playdates, after-school activities, or schedules. I needed to be connected to what was happening outside the hospital walls and also wanted to know how Griffin and Elyse were really handling and coping with everything.

At around 8:30 p.m., I would go to Bryan's room for the final time of the day. I would again massage his arms, hands, legs, and feet. I would tell him I loved him, I was right down the hall, and would see him in the morning. A gentle kiss goodnight and I'd be on my way back to the family room. I'd get my loveseat ready with sheets and blankets one of the ICU nurses had given us. I had chosen the loveseat that would allow me to see out into the hallway. I thought that, if I was here, I would be able to hear or see if anyone was coming to get me. Even if I was sleeping, the nurses could easily find me.

Before bed, I would write a CaringBridge update. There were so many people following our story and waiting for the next update. I was very open about what was happening to Bryan, and writing about our day and Bryan's status was very therapeutic for me. I always ended with specific things I needed everyone to pray for and a huge thank you to everyone for the support and love. People were able to live the journey with me.

After each post, I would read and reread all the words of encouragement that people wrote back. I needed to hear, "You are so strong," "Bryan is so lucky to have you there," "Bryan is a fighter" . . . It replenished my soul. Those words gave me strength to keep going.

I also started journaling. Every night, I would write down all the events of the day. Things were happening at a lightning-fast pace; I thought it would be a good idea to keep track of everything that was occurring, not only for me to look back on, but to be able to tell the kids and hopefully, one day, Bryan.

Getting ready for bed was my favorite time of day. I could breathe a sigh of relief because Bryan made it through another day. Nighttime was when I could escape from my nightmare of daytime filled with stress, anxiety, and fear. When I laid my head down, the exhaustion of the day was released and I was out. I took comfort in knowing my friends were going to check on Bryan throughout the night and would wake me if something was wrong.

A little more than a week after the accident, the Dakota County sheriff stopped by to tell me that they were still searching for the person who hit Bryan, but there were no solid leads. With the help of Bryan's company, along with my parents and Bryan's parents, the reward money had been increased to eleven thousand dollars. They would be sending Bryan's bicycle in for ballistic testing. If there was any transfer of paint from the vehicle to Bryan's bike, they would be able to determine the make and model of the vehicle. It would be a huge break in the case, since there was really no evidence at the scene. There were not even skid marks for the investigators to be able to reenact the scene. Getting the make and model of the vehicle would at least narrow the search.

I really didn't care about the investigation. My focus and energy had to be on Bryan. Finding out who hit him was not going to change what happened to Bryan. It wasn't going to change what we were going through. I knew I had to let this part of the accident go and let the investigators and others deal with it. If I got sucked into the negative, it would take me in a downward spiral that I couldn't afford to emotionally go down. I needed to focus on Bryan and the kids. Eventually, it would be nice to know how or why the accident happened, but thinking about that was for a later time.

Ten days after the accident, my workout partner, Jaleh, called to tell me that she and some coworkers were discussing Bryan's accident. One of her coworkers said, "My friend, Terry, was one of the first people on that accident scene."

I couldn't believe it. I might get some answers to what happened. "Jaleh, get me her number. I have to talk to her." *It's a small world indeed.*

I called Terry immediately. She described how she was traveling west on 250th Street, the opposite direction Bryan would have been traveling. The person in front of her stopped and pulled over, so she did, as well. There was a bike in the middle of the road.

"We had gotten out to move the bike when we saw Bryan. He was lying on the opposite side of the road. His helmet was still on, just a little cockeyed. A nurse and her boyfriend were the next people on the scene. The nurse held Bryan's head between her knees. Bryan was unconscious but moaning and moving his leg."

I didn't want to picture Bryan that way, in so much pain.

"The nurse unbuckled his helmet strap so it wouldn't restrict his airway but left the helmet in place. Someone found the baggie that had Bryan's wallet and phone. They looked at his driver's license so they could call him by his name. They were hoping this would calm him. They put blankets and a jacket over him to keep him warm. Another person came and prayed over him."

It was comforting to hear what happened at the scene and to realize there were so many people looking out for Bryan. I really couldn't envision what the accident scene looked like or imagine coming upon an accident like that. The main thing that I was ecstatic to hear was that Bryan had been moving his leg! He wasn't paralyzed at the accident scene. Hallelujah! I hoped and prayed that, because the nurse at the scene kept Bryan's head immobilized and didn't let anyone move him, it lessened the likelihood that he was paralyzed now.

Chapter 12

My mom and dad took on the parental role for Griffin and Elyse since they arrived in town. I talked to the kids almost every night but had only seen them three times since I walked out of the door to go to the hospital eleven days earlier. There were a lot of factors that prevented me from seeing them: they were back at school, both kids were in after-school activities, the Rush hour traffic, Bryan's condition was still in too critical.

To be honest, I wasn't worried about the kids. They were at school for most of the day, and I was at my new job as Bryan's caretaker. Griffin and Elyse would be in the best of hands with my parents. They would have the kids read and do their homework every night, get to bed at a decent time, and be loved the only way grandparents can.

People were being so generous to our family. They were thinking of so many ways to help us. Usually people think of furnishing a meal for a family in need. Spaghetti pie, garlic bread, salad, and cookie brownies were my go-to dishes for such occasions. Carmen set up a food train to have meals brought three days a week. This was a welcome blessing for my parents. A cooler was left on the front steps so people could deliver the meal at any time. It helped alleviate going to the grocery store and making meals. It also freed them up so they had time to come and visit me when the kids were at school, run errands, and do typical household things such as laundry, dishes, etc.

Moms & Neighbors (M&N), a non-profit organization, delivered breakfast foods every two weeks to our family. They knew the evening meals were being taken care of, so they thought breakfast foods would be a great idea. I had been a part of the organization for almost five years and was the current secretary. I was drawn to M&N because the organization was one hundred percent volunteer based. This allowed 99.7% of the money they raised, to go directly to families and teens in need in District 196 (Apple Valley, Rosemount, Eagan). M&N's motto was "The Power of Kindness." M&N wanted people to know that they weren't alone in their journey. I loved knowing that we were helping people right in our community, and my kids understood that we could be helping someone sitting right next to them in class. I always said, "You never know when you might be the one who needs help." *Full circle . . . now my family needs the help.*

Just when we thought we had it all covered, MHC, Bryan's workplace, came up with a wonderful generous and helpful gift. They paid to have the house cleaned every two weeks.

Playdates became a way for Elyse and Griffin's friends to help out. This provided a fun escape for the kids and to make things feel normal, so normal that one of the moms sent me the following message after talking with Elyse during a playdate: "My mom is at the hospital because my dad got hit by a car and now he is yellow AND he poops in a bag. She is now singing 'Baby Got Back.'" We had many laughs about this statement. I would expect nothing less from Elyse. She is my straightforward kid who tells it like it is. I was relieved she was taking it all in stride.

I had been counting down the days until the kids' spring break. Since I had hardly seen them since leaving the house that fateful night, I was hoping that they would get to come and spend tons of time with me at the hospital.

The North Memorial ICU family lounge was just about the furthest thing from the beaches of Puerto Vallarta, but it was going to have to do.

Erica and my nieces had the same spring break, so instead of going to Florida, they came to Eagan for the week. Erica stayed with me at the hospital, and this gave Shani a much-needed break. I'm not going to lie; I was a bit nervous having just Erica with me. We were both clueless on medical stuff, so if something happened, I wouldn't have Shani there to talk me through the situation.

My nieces, Morgan and Ingrid, stayed with my parents and kids. Even though they were older than Griffin and Elyse, they loved to be with them. A lot of activities were planned, thanks in part to a group of former students and other Red Pine families. They generously collected money for the kids to use at the water park, go bowling, ride the rides at the Mall of America, etc. They wanted the kids to have some fun during their spring break.

Twelve days after the accident and the first day of spring break, I decided it was time to have the kids come to the hospital for the first time. I hadn't wanted them to come sooner and see Bryan with tubes, machines, and the ventilator down his throat. The ventilator had covered the lower half of his face below his nose, so all you saw were Bryan's partially open, bulging eyes with an empty stare. If it weren't for all the machines beeping, you would have thought he was dead.

But Bryan had surgery the day before to put in a tracheostomy, as well as closing another inch or two of his abdomen. The tracheostomy was a cut in the throat, below the vocal cords, so a tube could be placed in his windpipe. The ventilator would now be attached to the trach. It was protocol to replace a regular ventilator after one or two weeks with a trach ventilator to prevent infection, like pneumonia. Now that Bryan had a trach, it was easier to cover his body up with a blanket, which would hide all the tubes and drains. The kids would be able to see Bryan's whole face except for the small cloth covering his eyes. It looked as if he were just sleeping. There wasn't anything else for me to do to make Bryan look better. The kids needed to see their dad. I had waited long enough.

Before I took Griffin and Elyse down the hall to Bryan's room, I showed them my temporary home where I slept and went to the bathroom. "Look at all the goodies that people have sent for us to snack on."

"Can we have some?"

"Help yourself."

After some nervous chitchat, I couldn't hold off the inevitable any longer. "Are you ready to go back and see your dad?" I asked them.

"I'm scared," Griffin said, burying his head in my side.

"Me too," said Elyse, coming over to sit by me.

"I know. Dad just looks like he is sleeping. I have blankets pulled up to his neck, and his eyes are covered. There are lots of machines on both sides of the bed, but they are all there to help Dad."

"I don't want to go," Griffin said with tears starting to well up.

"You don't have to go in the room. It will be just as if we went into either of your rooms at home and opened the door to look in. We will do that with Dad's room, but instead of a door, he has a sliding glass door. The nurses tell me that, even when he is sleeping, he can still hear us talking. I think he would love to hear your voices."

Slowly, very slowly, we made our way down the hall. As we got closer, I could feel them both start to shake. I put my arms around them and guided them to the threshold of Bryan's room. Standing at the threshold, the kids were at the foot of Bryan's bed looking directly at him. I wondered what was going through their minds as I watched their eyes grow bigger and bigger with horror. Could they see it was their dad? They both squeaked out a hushed "hi." Then they turned and ran back to the lounge with me chasing after them.

By the time I got to the lounge, Griffin was wrapped in my mom's arms, wailing. With tears in my eyes, I picked him up and brought him into the hall trying to calm him. Elyse quietly followed behind. I sat and held Griffin as Elyse snuggled by my side.

"Will Dad be OK? Is he going to be the same?" Griffin asked.

"I don't really know. I hope so. The nurses and doctors are doing everything they can." I didn't want to lie to him.

"I don't want to see Dad again. I'm too scared. He's never going to be the same."

Elyse nodded her head in agreement.

What do I say to them? I didn't know if Bryan would ever be the same. I hoped beyond hope that this nightmare would be over and he would be able to play with Griffin and Elyse like he always did. But I didn't know what he'd be able to do.

"You don't have to see him again today. You both did a great job. I am sure Dad would be so proud of you. You know Dad is a fighter and he is going to give his all. We have to continue to be strong, too."

We spent a half hour or so in the hallway together and then went and joined the others in the lounge.

Shortly after, a man walked into our side of the family lounge with an edible fruit bouquet. He asked, "Are you Shauna Joas?" He gave his name and told us he had been following our story in the news and on CaringBridge. He just wanted us to know that we were in his thoughts and he was wishing us well. It took me a while to realize the fruit bouquet was from him. I thought he was the delivery guy. I was dumbfounded to think that some stranger would do that for us. I thanked and thanked him. He just smiled and walked away. There are such good people in the world. This was one of the many examples of kindness that was bestowed on us.

The bouquet was almost too beautiful to eat, but after we were done eating what we could, I decided to take what was left to the nurses' station. It was my hope that, if we treated the nurses well and gave them a little extra, they may have a little more time and patience for Bryan. I was shocked that Griffin followed me and asked, "Can I say goodbye to Dad?"

"Of course!"

Griffin stood at the threshold of the room and waved. My heart broke for him. Bryan was his buddy, the one who played football, hockey, lacrosse, and rough house with him. *Would things ever be like that again?*

I knew it was time for the kids to leave, so I put on my fake smile, hiding from them how hard it was for me to say goodbye. Hand in hand, we walked slowly down the hall to the elevators, trying to prolong the inevitable for as long as possible. "Love you both. Please be good for Meme and Papa. Have fun with Morgan and Ingrid."

"We will, Mom."

"Thank you for being so brave today. I am so proud of you both. I love you."

"Love you too, Mom."

With one last hug and kiss, I watched them walk into the elevator with my mom and dad, waving until the doors closed. Then I collapsed against the wall by the elevators and sobbed as I watched the numbers on the elevator reach the first floor. They were gone . . . going home, and I had to go back to my home down the hall.

Am I doing the right thing staying here twenty-four seven and not being with my kids during this upheaval in our lives? Not only is Bryan in the hospital and fighting to live, but I'm gone from them, too.

I was blessed to have the love and support of my parents to care for the kids. There was nothing more I wanted to do than to run after them, take them home, and forget about this nightmare. But I knew in my heart that I needed to be Bryan's voice. He couldn't speak for himself or make decisions. I had to be the one. This was where I needed to be.

Chapter 13

For thirteen days, only the machines were telling me that Bryan was alive, but now I had seen some movements. He was moving his head from side to side, scrunching his face, puckering his lips, trying to lift his arm, and scraping his teeth across the big gauge he had in his tongue from almost biting it in half. Bryan's tongue never was stitched, so he has a permanent two-inch gash across the top of his tongue about an inch from the tip. *Oh my God! He really is alive. Bryan is coming back to me. Once he wakes up, everything will be fine. Maybe we will get to go home.*

"I can't believe Bryan is finally waking up. He is doing these weird facial movements and popping noises with his lips," I said to the nurse when she came in. "It looks like he's in pain."

"Those are definitely interesting movements," the nurse said.

The doctors soon discovered that some of Bryan's movements were due to an allergic reaction to the medication Reglan, which is a medication used to treat and prevent vomiting and nausea. The doctors were hoping the medicine would help Bryan be able to keep the nutrition down, allowing it time to go through his system, but now that medicine would have to be stopped immediately.

I am not sure how they determined it was Reglan that Bryan was allergic to, but once it was stopped, all of Bryan's weird movements faded, leaving behind very few natural ones. How could that be? He had been shrugging his shoulders, scrunching his nose, making noises with his lips, moving his head so much that he wore off all the hair on the back of his head . . . How could that not be real? The wind was knocked out of my sails.

Then Bryan developed a bit of a fever, which terrified me and sent me further into a tailspin. You always hear about people dying from an infection, not what actually put them in the hospital in the first place. The nurses tried not to give him any Tylenol because it was hard on the liver. Bryan's liver counts were still continuing to rise, and he was so yellow it was as if he was almost glowing. The doctors sent Bryan's liver tests over to the University of Minnesota for a consultation. The university is the place that does liver transplants and has experts in this field. North Memorial wanted to make sure they weren't missing anything. After reviewing his test, the University of Minnesota specialists said all of his liver numbers were consistent with a trauma. There were no signs of blockage or severe damage.

Fourteen days after the accident, it was a major surgery day with two separate operations back to back. Dr. Farhat would be closing Bryan's abdominal muscles completely. Then, Dr. Woods, the orthopedic doctor, would do surgery on Bryan's pelvis. She looked young. I was getting older, so everyone looked young to me. But she was very thorough in her explanation, which gave me full confidence in her.

She had held off the surgery until Bryan was a bit more stable. Now that Bryan was starting to move a little, Dr. Woods wanted to get his pelvis stabilized before there was permanent damage that couldn't be repaired. The sacrum, which is the large triangular bone at the base of the spine, was broken, allowing the left side of his pelvis to be completely ripped away from the right side. Both of his hip sockets were broken, too. When Dr. Woods initially looked at his scans, she thought she would have to do multiple surgeries to fix everything. Today, the plan was to fix the sacrum. Because Bryan was non-weight bearing, the broken bones in his back would heal on their own. That was positive news of one less thing to cut into Bryan to have repaired, but the doctor warned me that the sacrum surgery alone could last anywhere from six to nine hours.

His surgery was scheduled for 12:30 p.m., and Erica, Shelly, and I went to wish Bryan good luck. When I was giving him a kiss and squeezing his hand three times, which meant "I love you," I felt a small squeeze back. My heart melted. *Does he know I am there, or is it just a reflex?* I'd like to think he knew it was me. "Honey, you've got this. I will see you when you get back to your room," I whispered in his ear.

Then the waiting began. After three hours, Dr. Farhat's part of the surgery was done. He came into the lounge to give us an update. "I closed Bryan's abdomen. The fluid in his abdomen was a little dirty, so I spent some time cleaning it out. I put some drains in to make sure if there is any infection, it will drain out. Antibiotics will be started as soon as he is out of surgery."

Dirty . . . not the word I wanted to hear used about Bryan's insides. My panic ramped up again. All I could do was trust that Dr. Farhat cleaned it all out and the antibiotics would kill any nasty germs that were still lingering. *Please God, this is enough.* Now, we waited for Dr. Woods.

Thank goodness Erica and Shelly were with me. They did their best to try and keep my spirits up. We walked the halls, ate snacks, checked Facebook and CaringBridge, even took a few catnaps. I wished I could hit the fast-forward button, but time seemed to be stuck in slow motion.

Later in the evening, my good friends Jenny and Angie came to bring dinner and stay for the night too. It would be just like a slumber party. The three of us had a lot to talk and laugh about. We had been friends for many years. Jenny and I were roommates in college, and Angie joined us when we all got hired the same year, back in 1999, at the same school.

Around 7:30 p.m., seven hours after surgery began, Dr. Woods finally came into the family lounge to tell me about her surgery. "Bryan is still in the operating room. They are getting him ready to take him back to his room. I am very happy with how his surgery went. I put two screws in the back of Bryan's pelvis to connect the sides together. The front of the pelvis lined up nicely with the closing of the back side. This is the only surgery I'll do. With all of the surgeries on Bryan's abdomen region, I am not going to touch the front of his pelvis. There is just too much risk for infection. I am pleased with how well the pelvis came together. It's good enough. He may get arthritis a little faster, but that is the least of his worries. His hip sockets will just heal on their own."

I was numb from sitting for all that time and worrying. The outcome for the day had been somewhat positive, and I'll consider it that we won the day. "Thank you for everything, Dr. Woods."

Not so fast, when Bryan got back from surgery, his blood pressure dropped significantly, so he had to be put back on two vassal compressors. Hopefully, this was a temporary thing. Shelly decided to stay an extra night because Bryan was so unstable after surgery, and I was so grateful that she was there. Whenever Shelly and/or Shani were there, I relaxed a little because their medical knowledge eased my mind. They could read Bryan's numbers, hear what the doctors and nurses were saying, inspect his drains, and tell me what was happening. I know they didn't tell me everything, especially if they were worried, but they told me what they thought I needed to know. When they weren't there, I would panic about everything owing to my lack of medical knowledge and uncertainties.

The next morning, I dreaded going down the hall. *How did the rest of Bryan's night go? What would this day bring?* As I rounded the corner, Bryan seemed stable. He looked like he was resting peacefully.

"Bryan had a rough night," the nurse said, which I wasn't expecting. "At 1:00 a.m., his blood levels were off the charts, so we needed to do an emergency round of dialysis, which helped stabilize him. His blood pressure leveled out, so the vassal compressors have been stopped. He is doing much better now."

Poor Bryan. *How much more can he take?* I can't believe all of that happened with me right down the hall as I slept. But things were OK now, I reminded myself. I felt guilty that he had to go through all that without someone there with him, while I slept.

I was starting to do my ritual of massaging his arms and legs when I thought I saw movement in his legs. I never had seen Bryan's legs move, even during the allergic reaction movements. The accident scene reports stated Bryan had leg movement, how could I be sure something didn't happen in the transportation to the hospital or the surgeries themselves? I froze and held my breath, waiting, watching, praying that they would move again. After what seemed like an eternity, they moved again. He wasn't paralyzed. I had tried not to worry about paralysis the last fifteen days, but it had crept into my mind if I let it. *What would paralysis mean for our future? A new home that is handicap accessible? A different car? In-home care?* Could I now let that worry go?

"We are going to try to wean Bryan off the ventilator today," one of the nurses said.

What? How is that possible? He was so unstable last night; now they are going to disconnect him from the ventilator that was keeping him alive?

"He has been breathing over the ventilator, which means he was taking breaths on his own in addition to what the machine was doing for him. This tells us that he is ready to be weaned."

How are they going to know if it doesn't work? Will he feel like he is suffocating? Put your trust in the staff. They know what they are doing.

Erica and I planned to go back to the house and see the kids. Shelly was going to stay with Bryan until we got back. I really didn't want to be there when they took him off the ventilator. I know this contradicts why I was staying at the hospital. I didn't know what to expect. My mind turned it into something scary. I envisioned him gasping for breath and struggling. I knew the ventilator was keeping him alive. When they took him off, would he desperately be trying to breathe, stop breathing, and then die? It was something I didn't want to witness. I was so grateful Shelly was there; she was actually giddy about him being removed from the vent.

Bryan's temperature was not on the monitors, but Shelly felt like his fever was down. She also checked his drain tubes and said they looked good. "He's doing much better, Shauna," she reassured me. "You can go. I will call you if anything happens."

This was still spring break week, and with Morgan and Ingrid staying, the kids were having fun and didn't want to visit. I understood but was disappointed, too. I didn't blame them—what kids would want to come to a place that terrified them when they could be having a blast with their cousins and getting to do things that I usually wouldn't let them do? None.

Erica and I headed home to shower and to see the kids. It had been five days since my last shower. I couldn't wait to have a few minutes to myself, no beeping machines or hospital smell, no trying to keep a smile on my face. I could let my guard down and shed tears of sadness and anxiety that I kept locked inside.

Griffin, Elyse, Morgan, and Ingrid were at Grand Slam with my parents and arrived home as I was just finishing getting ready. It brought me such joy listening to Griffin and Elyse go on and on about how much fun they had.

"We got to jump on the trampolines, drive the bumper cars, and play video games," Elyse said. "I got lots of tickets and used them to buy three pieces of candy and this cool squishy green frog." They were being "normal" kids when their lives were not "normal."

Griffin added, "I won lots of tickets, too. I got candy and this soft baseball. We had so much fun!"

"It sounds like it," I told them. "Aunt Erica and I have to get back to the hospital. Maybe Meme and Papa will bring you there later today or tomorrow. Come here so I can give you both a hug goodbye." Then Erica and I were off. I had to relish the times I was with them, even if it was brief. Bryan's accident had been fifteen days ago, and I had seen the kids three times. The doctors were still on a day-to-day basis with Bryan with no indication of a next step. They were my inspiration for hope. All of their energy and joy replenished my bucket to face another day.

When Erica and I returned to the hospital, they had turned off Bryan's ventilator. There was no machine noise forcing the air into his lungs, just his own sweet breath. "How long has he been breathing on his own?" I asked.

"A couple of hours," Shelly answered. "Bryan did awesome. There were no concerns."

Usually when someone was being weaned, they slowly turned down the amount of support from the machine that was helping a person to breathe. They let the patient breathe on their own for a bit and then turn the ventilator back on because the patient will become too exhausted and need assistance. Astonishingly, once Bryan's ventilator was turned off and he was breathing on his own, they never had to turn it back on. The ventilator was still connected just in case. Bryan was still in a coma, a state of unconsciousness where a person is unresponsive and cannot be woken, but now breathing on his own. These past two days were such an emotional roller coaster. The highs were amazing. You could almost glimpse the finish line after running a marathon, but then the spirits would drop when you realized you were only halfway through, still unsure if you will be able to finish. In twenty-four hours, Bryan had a huge surgery, emergency dialysis, and now was breathing on his own.

It felt like when I might be able to take a deep breath, a kick in the stomach was just around the corner. This was my constant worry. Things would look up and then—*BAM*, something else would go wrong. If you let your emotional guard down for an instant, it makes the setbacks much harder to deal with.

The following day, my parents took Griffin, Elyse, Morgan, and Ingrid to go on rides at the Mall of America and go shopping. Another "not normal" day for the kids but a positive one. Griffin started complaining of his head hurting, was coughing, and wanted to lie down on any bench he saw. My mom took him to the doctor the next day, and he was diagnosed with influenza A and pneumonia.

The doctor gave a prescription for medicine for Elyse also. "If Elyse comes down with the same symptoms, it is more likely she would have influenza A, too," the doctor told my mom.

Therefore, they were all banned from the hospital for a few days to give the medicine a chance to work. Now I wouldn't be able to see them. I felt sorry for myself. I was so looking forward to spending more time with them, even if it was at the hospital. I had pictured us playing games, watching movies, stopping in to see Bryan, just being together. I couldn't get sick, and Bryan definitely couldn't. Poor Griffin.

I remember when I was little and sick; all I wanted was my mom or dad to take care of me. They always made me feel better. And now neither Bryan nor I would be there. It broke my heart, but I knew my parents would give the same care as they had given me. Griffin would be OK.

After a few days, Griffin was feeling better and no longer had a fever. So they went to a movie and then came up to visit. Everyone wore masks. As we were sitting in the lounge, Elyse fell asleep. This was very unusual for her. She never took naps. She could watch a movie late at night and be the only one still awake at the end. I felt her forehead. She was burning up. Shit. The ban was reinstated. They left immediately.

Shani bought an essential oil diffuser. We put in a germ fighter oil, made of lemon, clove bud, eucalyptus, cinnamon, rosemary, and cineole. It was designed to support the immune system in fighting off germs, providing you relief, and keeping you in good health. That was what we needed. I was willing to try anything to help Bryan. Even if it didn't help, the oil had a fantastic fresh smell, which masked the hospital room odors. Anyone who has been in a hospital knows the hospital smell. The nurses and doctors loved the diffuser, too.

Bryan continued to become more alert and was continuing to do well off the ventilator. But I was anxious. I didn't realize it took so long to "wake up." It definitely was not like you see in the movies where the person opened their eyes and everything was back to normal. Bryan's eyes would be open for brief periods of time with a bit of movement in his body, shaking his head yes or no or squeezing my hand. He just needed more time.

Every day, the neurologist had been coming in to assess Bryan to try to determine if he had a brain injury. There was a small spot on his brain they had detected initially, but the neurologist was unable to make an accurate diagnosis since Bryan was still in a coma. Now that Bryan was slowly waking up and could follow simple commands, assessing him was easier. All signs so far indicated that Bryan had no signs of a brain injury. It was incredible. I can't say enough about the importance of helmets. Bryan got hit by a speeding vehicle and didn't have a traumatic brain injury. *How is that even possible?* Another miracle.

The first real acknowledgement I had of Bryan knowing I was there came seventeen days after the nightmare began. I had already massaged Bryan's arms and legs, and I sat in the folding chair holding Bryan's hand for a bit before bedtime. "I'm going to go to bed. I will be right down the hall. I love you, Bryan."

He mouthed, "I love you."

I couldn't answer back. Tears were streaming down my face. *Did he really mouth that? Was it my imagination?* Words I longed to hear. It had been seventeen long, exhausting, turbulent days of day-after-day caring for Bryan without any true indication that he knew I was with him. He had no idea what we had gone through for seventeen days. I'd had to make life-and-death decisions for him. I was living at the hospital, sleeping in a loveseat, while my parents had taken over caring for our kids. He was still really sick. But he knew I was there, and I knew he was there. Seeing his love for me made my heart burst. Everything had been worth it, and we would continue to fight. No low on this roller coaster ride could ever take away the high of the mouthed "I love you."

Chapter 14

Griffin's tenth birthday was nineteen days after the accident. A friend that I work with asked if she could get Griffin a cake. It had always been Bryan's job to make the kids' birthday cakes.

That tradition started a few weeks before Griffin's first birthday. "What kind of cake are you going to make Griffin?" Bryan asked me.

"Um, Cub Foods," I replied.

"My mom always made me my cakes."

I wasn't a cake baker, and I certainly didn't have time to add it to the party-prep list. "Well, if you think Griffin needs a homemade cake, you will have to make it yourself."

And so began the birthday cake tradition. Bryan didn't just make a sheet cake. He used cake, Rice Krispy treats, and homemade fondant frosting to sculpt masterpieces. Over the years, he made the Star Wars Death Star and battleship, 3D dogs, three-foot hockey stick with puck, and Olaf from the movie *Frozen*.

My coworker, Jessica, found a baker, Weezie, from Rosemount, Minnesota. She said she could make a lacrosse stick cake, which would be very "Bryan like." Another coincidence was that Weezie's daughter was friends with some of the University of Minnesota lacrosse players. After Weezie told the players our story, she asked if they would be willing to deliver the cake to Griffin. They wholeheartedly agreed.

The morning of Griffin's birthday, another one of Bryan's racing buddies, Jiggy, came to watch Bryan so I could go home for the afternoon and be a part of the celebration. Griffin knew the neighborhood kids were going to come over for pizza and cake at noon but had no idea the Gopher players were coming.

At 1:00 p.m., a truck pulled up, and five gopher players got out. They carried the lacrosse stick cake up the driveway. I literally had to push Griffin out the door to meet the guys. He had no idea what was going on or who these strangers were. I followed him with my camera on hand. "Griffin, these guys are lacrosse players that play for the Gophers," I told him.

"What?" Griffin was shocked.

"Hey, Griffin. Happy Birthday," all the players said.

"Thank you," Griffin said shyly.

They had a few gifts to give Griffin: a pinnie signed by the team, a pair of Gopher lacrosse sweatpants, and shorts. For Bryan, they had a Gopher lacrosse polo shirt. What a thoughtful gesture.

After we took a few pictures of Griffin and the players, we gathered everyone outside for cake. The players helped us sing "Happy Birthday" to Griffin and stayed for cake.

Once the cake was done, one of the players asked if anyone wanted to play some lacrosse. Of course, they did. The kids ran home and grabbed their sticks. Griffin set up his nets, and the game began.

This last-minute party exceeded all my expectations. The cake was perfect. I saw the bright Griffin smile with sparkling eyes appear that had been absent since the accident. It was such an amazing surprise for him.

The Gopher players were such stand-up young men. They ended up staying for two hours. I think they would have stayed longer, but they had a game that night.

After everyone left, I pulled Griffin aside to give him his birthday presents from Bryan and me. Bryan had been so excited to surprise Griffin with Oakley sunglasses. When he opened the box and saw the Oakleys, he couldn't stop crying. I told him that it had been Dad's idea and they were bought before the accident.

I didn't want this day to end, but I had been gone over five hours, the longest I had been away from Bryan. I started feeling that invisible pull from the hospital telling me it was time to go back. "It was such a memorable day, Griffin, one you will never forget."

"I only wish Dad could have been here," Griffin said as he reached for a hug.

"Me too, Griff," I said squeezing him tighter. "I should really get back to him. I have been gone a long time. I wouldn't have missed this day for anything. I hope you liked your surprise."

"It was awesome," he said.

"Elyse," I called, "I have to go."

"Bye, Mom," Elyse said as she ran to give me a hug.

"I will see you tomorrow at the hospital. We are going to celebrate Easter there. Shani and Shelly are going to make us all lunch," I explained.

After I got back to the hospital, I received a message on Facebook from one of the officers that had come to our house the night of Bryan's accident. We had been in contact a few times since that night.

"I hope Griffin's birthday is going well considering how stressful things have been," wrote Sergeant Anselment. "My partner Jen and I are both working tonight (we were the ones that came to your house that awful night.) Would it be OK if we dropped off a gift for Griffin . . .? I realize he may associate us with bad news, and I wouldn't want to make things worse. We have something for Elyse too."

"That would be fine. I'll let my parents know. Thank you so much!" I answered back.

"We will be there around 7:00-ish."

"Perfect."

I let my parents know so that they would be prepared. At 7:00 p.m., the doorbell rang and my mom went to the door. She called to Griffin, "Griffin, come here. You have a surprise! There are some people here that want to wish you a happy birthday."

Griffin came running around the corner and abruptly stopped when he saw the police officers standing there.

"Hi, Griffin, I am Sergeant Anselment and this is Sergeant Wegner. We were with you the night of your dad's accident."

"I know," Griffin timidly said.

"These are for you," they said as they handed him a balloon bouquet of six mylar balloons. They must have bought every balloon that said "Happy Birthday" on it. Griffin's fear slowly faded. "We hope you are having a happy birthday."

"I am. I had a party and the Gopher lacrosse players came. My mom was here, too."

They handed each of the kids a gift bag filled with a gift card to Dairy Queen, movie passes, and candy.

"We have to be on our way because we are on duty. Thanks for letting us stop by."

"Thank you for the gifts," both the kids said.

This was an amazing gesture and went way beyond the call of duty. They showed my children what it meant to be a police officer. The impression they made on my kids will have lifelong effects.

The day after Griffin's birthday was Easter. The kids' morning began with the discovery of colorful eggs hidden all over the front and side yard. They grabbed empty ice cream buckets from the garage and ran around collecting the eggs from their hiding places in the bushes, flowerbeds, and rock wall. To this day, we still don't know who did this. It was another amazing surprise that Griffin and Elyse experienced at the hands of some mystery angels. *Could the Easter bunny be real?*

Bryan began his Easter morning with dialysis. Then the nurse shaved him and washed his hair so he would be Easter ready.

There are these amazing shower caps that have shampoo and conditioner in them. The cap was heated up and then put on Bryan's head, where you massaged his scalp for a few minutes. Then you take the cap off, towel dry his hair, and it is done. No water needed.

Instead of getting dressed up, going to church, having a ham dinner with all the fixings around the dining room table, we would be at the hospital. There would be twelve of us: Griffin, Elyse, my parents, Shani and Mike, Gregg, Shelly, and their son Wyatt, and Bryan's parents. We all crammed into our side of the lounge, using paper plates, dishing food out of crock pots, and balancing our plates on our knees.

Shani and Shelly planned and made Easter dinner. They not only had enough to feed the twelve of us, but enough for the entire ICU staff. There was ham, potatoes, rolls, veggies, salad, cheese and crackers, and some gooey peanut butter brownies. The only thing that mattered that day was that we were together.

The ICU staff would come down when they had a break to grab a plate of food. They were grateful to have a little Easter celebration, too.

Gregg and Mike took the kids to the park in the back of the hospital to play. They played soccer and lacrosse and chased around Gregg and Shelly's dog, Dave. We watched them from the family lounge window. It was good to see them run around laughing and having fun, but at the same time, it was difficult to watch. Bryan should have been out there playing with them, not lying in the ICU, fighting to recover.

Griffin went to see Bryan once. We wouldn't let Elyse go back with him, since she had a slight fever the day before. We needed to be extra cautious that Bryan was not exposed to any germs. Griffin wouldn't go into the room but stood at the threshold where he felt most comfortable.

"Hi, Dad."

With a smile, Bryan waved to Griffin for the first time.

"Love you," said Griffin.

Bryan's head nodded and a silent "I love you, too" moved across his lips.

"Bye, Dad."

Bryan raised his arm enough to give a small wave back.

I told Bryan, "I'll be back. I am going to say goodbye to the kids."

As we started walking down the hall, Griffin turned to me. "Mom," he said beaming, "Dad waved to me. He's getting better."

"He is. Dad is working really hard to get stronger."

There was nothing normal about the celebrations the last two days, but yet, they were celebrations I would never forget. Being surrounded by family and friends brought joy and laughter back to my world. They reminded me that there was so much to celebrate. Bryan was still with us and making his comeback. As Jesus rose from the dead on Easter, Bryan was having his own resurrection from what looked like his deathbed—*our Easter miracle.*

The tube feedings continued to be one disaster after another. Bryan either threw up, or the nutrients just sat in his stomach and had to be suctioned out. The doctors were determined to make the tube feedings work. The other feeding option, TPN (total parenteral nutrition), which gave nutrients directly into a person's bloodstream, was really hard on a person's kidneys and liver and had an increased infection risk. This wouldn't have been good for Bryan's kidneys and liver, since neither were functioning properly. He needed nutrients to heal and function. You could see the frustration in the doctors' faces. TPN was going to be a last resort. *How long can Bryan go without getting any nutrition? His once tree-trunk, muscular legs have dwindled to twigs. How can Bryan's bones and body heal without getting the proper nutrients into his system?*

After twenty-two days, the doctors couldn't wait any longer, so they reluctantly started TPN. I had mixed feelings about it. I was thrilled that he was getting fed, but knowing how apprehensive the doctors were made me feel uneasy. I hoped this was the right decision, because it would be his lifeline. I prayed that it wouldn't do anymore damage to his fragile liver and kidneys.

Bryan had his eyes open for longer periods of time and was trying to interact with people by grabbing people by the hand, waving, mouthing words, and following commands. He was not sleeping very much. The nurses would tell me that Bryan was awake all night. The lights were dimmed in the ICU area, but the constant sounds and movements of the ICU area continued. Bryan was extremely sensitive to the tiniest of these: the beeping of the machines, the opening and closing of the door to his room, the phone ringing, the nurses chatting, the changing of Bryan's position to prevent bed sores, and on and on. It seemed as if he was on high alert all the time, always looking around and checking things out. You would think he was finally asleep, but with any movement or noise, his eyes opened.

He tried to mouth words, but with a trach, you need a Passy-Muir valve to actually speak. You put the valve on the end of the trach to redirect air flow through the vocal folds, mouth, and nose, enabling a person to speak.

Bryan hadn't been able to produce any sounds yet. He would just mouth words but would become very frustrated when I couldn't understand what he was trying to tell me. The only word I could figure out was "whatever," which he said often.

I tried to have him write on a whiteboard, but he was too weak. The marker would just slip out of his fingers. The occupational therapist (OT) had Bryan squeezing rectangle sponges of different resistances to work on his strength and lift one- or three-pound weights. From the look in Bryan's eyes, I could tell he was embarrassed, frustrated, and in disbelief by this. He went from one-hundred-mile bike rides most weekends to squeezing sponges.

Bryan only had the valve put on when the speech therapist came in. The speech therapist always began with making Bryan hum. Bryan would hesitantly put on the valve. He would hum a few times. Then I would see his eyes get big and fill with panic. He would frantically pull the valve off. You could see the instant relief once the valve came off. It seemed as if he was suffocating with the valve on. Many deep, calming breaths and lots of begging from me before he would be willing to try again. I knew he needed to practice and get used to using the valve, but it was torturous to see Bryan suffering. It was as if I were holding him underwater and not letting him up until the last second.

Carmen brought my mom up to visit for the afternoon, and we were sitting in the lounge when a nurse came running in. My heart dropped.

"What happened to Bryan?"

"Nothing bad. The physical therapist, Paul, was having Bryan sit up on the edge of the bed. I thought you would like to see this."

This was the first time Bryan had been upright in twenty-four days. We all went running to his room. There he was sitting up, with his legs dangling over the side of the bed, Paul squatting in front of him ready to catch him if he fell. When Bryan turned to look at me, I tried to hide my shock and hor-ror. He looked like a person from a concentration camp with his hollowed cheeks, bulging eyes, and big teeth. Bryan's gown had opened in the back. Every bone and rib were visible on his back. Bryan had been so swollen from his surgeries and retained so much water, I hadn't realized how skinny he had gotten. How could a person so physically fit atrophy so much in such a short time? I focused on the excitement of him being vertical. "This is amazing, Bryan. Look at you!"

He just smiled with tears in his eyes. He could only stay upright for a few minutes. The PT said that Bryan was doing much of the work himself, so it took a lot of energy.

Later that day, a package was delivered to Bryan's room. It was a beautiful handmade quilt from a local cyclist who had been following our story. Her husband had been involved in a hit-and-run riding home from work about a week after Bryan's accident. Luckily, he escaped with some broken bones, cuts, and bruises. She wanted us to feel the warmth and comfort of the support around us. She, along with many other fellow cyclists, were pulling for us. I would have never thought to send something to a stranger, but the thoughtfulness again rocked me to my core. It was the ultimate example of a pay-it-forward moment. I would think of all of their kind gestures for years to come.

When I settled in for the night and checked my messages before bed, I saw that my college friend, Kourtney, had messaged me. I hadn't spoken to Kourtney in years. She and I, along with Jenny, had gone through our education program together at the University of Wisconsin-Eau Claire. Kourtney had moved to the Green Bay, Wisconsin area after graduating to teach, and we had lost touch. She wanted to know if it would be all right to give my information to a motivational speaker whom one of her friends had heard speak before a marathon. The woman's name was Colleen Kelly Alexander.

Colleen is an athlete, motivational speaker, as well as an author. She had many serious medical issues that she has overcome—Chiari malformation in her brain, lupus, cryoglobulinemia—but the fight of her life came in

2011. Colleen was out on a routine bike ride and was run over by a freight truck. She was crushed, ripped apart, and bleeding out. She flatlined twice and spent five weeks in a coma. She defied insurmountable odds. She is back competing in triathlons.

"Of course," I wrote back to Kourtney, "I would love to talk with her."

Kourtney sent Colleen the following message on Facebook messenger: "I heard about you from a friend. I sent your name and story to a friend of mine whose husband was just hit by a car on his bicycle and ran over. He is still in the hospital. Please consider following his story. He and his family could use some inspiration right now. Thank you for your time . . ."

Kourtney heard back from Colleen within minutes. "Oh my goodness. Tears. Can I have their phone? I would love to call his wife."

A short time later, Colleen called me. She was so kind. She wanted to make sure I was OK. "We all bleed red," Colleen said. "We have to help each other. Remain strong. Anything I can help you with, please call."

After I hung up with Colleen, I sat for a minute and reflected on our phone call. I couldn't help but think: if she survived her injuries, which seemed way worse than Bryan's, he could survive, too. There was restored hope. Maybe someday we would be the ones who were calling to tell our story and give encouragement to someone who needs it through their journey.

Besides connecting me with Colleen, Kourtney had been posting updates of our story on her Facebook page. Kourtney's husband is an avid biker, so their group of friends were touched by our story and they felt compelled to help. Gift cards to Target, Subway, gas stations, along with VISA gift cards were gathered. Kourtney sent these along with cards and notes of encouragement from her network of friends, all strangers to me—another amazing example of people coming together to help. The kindness of strangers was abundant, a reminder that there was good in this world.

Stewy flew in from Dallas again. It was twenty-six days after the accident. He had been in constant contact with me since he left, but he needed to see Bryan's progress with his own eyes. The last time Stewy saw Bryan, seventeen days earlier, he was still on life support and in a coma.

"I can't wait for you to see Bryan," I said. "He has been a bit lethargic over the past few days because he hasn't been sleeping well. He hasn't actually spoken words because of the trach in his throat. But he can talk to you silently. You'll get good at lip reading."

"Anything will be better than how I left him," Stewy said.

When we stepped around the corner to Bryan's room, Bryan's face lit up with a huge smile and wide eyes.

"Hey, buddy," Stewy said as he hugged Bryan, "it is so good to see you."

Bryan slowly mouthed, "Why are you here?"

"I was here a few weeks ago, and I had to come back to see you."

"You were here?" Bryan's face creased in confusion.

"Of course, I was."

"I'll leave the two of you alone," I told Stewy. "He may doze off and on, but you need your time together."

"Thanks."

I went back to the lounge for some quiet time with Shelly, knowing Bryan was in good hands. "Shelly, you should have seen it," I said. "It was like long-lost friends seeing each other for the first time in years, even though it had only been a few weeks. You could see the happiness radiating from them. It was such an incredible moment to witness. Bryan and I sure are blessed with the love of friends like you and Gregg." I reached over to give her a hug.

Stewy came back to the lounge after spending a few hours with Bryan. He wanted to be with him even if it was in silence. That's what friends do.

We all were tired. It was time for bed. We went to say good night to Bryan, and then we found our "beds." As I was drifting off to sleep, I could hear Stewy talking to his wife, Tracy, on the phone. "You just wouldn't believe how incredible it was to see Bryan with his eyes open. He knows I am here. I am so glad I came. My buddy, Bryan, is on his way back. Tracy, he's on his way back . . ."

I couldn't stop the tears from filling my eyes.

The next morning, I quietly got up and went in to see Bryan around 7:00 a.m. to do my morning routine, massaging his legs and arms with lotion. He felt really warm. *Shit. Is another infection brewing? When is this going to end? Will I ever get to leave the Haunted House?*

As I passed the nurses' station on my way back to the lounge, I mentioned to them, "Bryan feels warm today."

"OK, we'll check on it."

About fifteen minutes later, Nurse Jackie came running into the family lounge. The dreadful look on her face told me she wasn't there to tell me something good.

"There was a code blue called on Bryan."

"A code blue? What is that?" I asked her.

"It is when a patient is having a medical emergency. Bryan has stopped breathing."

"What? I was just back there!" I was shocked. *How could this be happening? He was fine a few minutes ago. Why did he stop breathing?* Dread filled my body. I couldn't make myself go back to Bryan alone. The uncontrollable shaking set in. The anxiety pressure was crushing my chest. Panic-filled tears rolled down my cheeks. My mind went into a fog. "Stewy, where is Shelly? Bryan is coding. We have to get back there. I need both of you."

"I don't know where Shelly is. I'll go look for her," Stewy said as he took off running down the hall.

I stood there frozen, not moving. *How is this happening?* On one hand, I didn't want to witness Bryan struggling to stay alive, but on the other hand, I wanted him to know I was there for him and to comfort him if this was the end.

It seemed like forever, but Shelly stepped out of the bathroom at the same time Stewy was running back into the lounge.

"We were looking for you. They called a code blue on Bryan," I told her in a frenzy.

"What?" Shelly said.

"We have to go back there, but I am too scared. I don't think I can."

"We got you, Shauna," they told me.

Shelly and Stewy guided me back. They were on either side of me, propelling me forward. By the time we got back there, the emergency was over. The doctors and nurses who had desperately struggled to get him to breathe again had done their job and were slowly making their way out of the room. The backboard that had been placed under him in case CPR needed to be started was removed. Fortunately, CPR didn't have to be performed.

The trauma doctor in charge, Dr. Evans, spoke quietly to us. "A nurse pulled out the inner cannula of Bryan's trach and discovered it was plugged with mucus. We determined that the blocked trach is what caused the respiratory failure. Once the mucus plug was out, all of Bryan's stats started returning to normal. He had to be put back on the ventilator. I feel this will only be for a short time. We need to let Bryan's body rest after the trauma of the code." We hadn't had Dr. Evans as a doctor before. He was very tall with short blond hair and looked to be in his thirties. You could tell he was very knowledgeable, but his bedside manner was not the best—it was just the facts, no compassion.

"Thank you," I said. "I'm grateful Bryan is in good hands."

It was disheartening to see Bryan on the ventilator again. Such a step back. I hoped the doctor was correct and it would be just a temporary thing. Another crisis averted. *How do we keep getting so lucky?*

I had heard different colored codes announced over the hospital's PA system since arriving at the hospital. I knew they probably weren't a good thing but had never thought to ask what they were for. After Bryan's code blue for a medical emergency, I wanted to know what the other codes meant. I found on the Internet what each color signified. For example, code red is fire/smoke, code white is a violent/behavioral situation, code yellow is a missing person, etc.

From that point on, whenever I heard a code blue, I knew that someone was in an urgent situation where his/her life depended on the doctors and nurses. I hoped it wouldn't be Bryan, but now my heart went out to the anonymous patient and family members each time I heard a code blue.

As a follow-up, the doctor ordered a bronchoscopy, a chest X-ray, lab work, and a change in Bryan's central line location. Bryan continued to have a fever, and they were concerned he had something brewing in his lower lung. They were also going to switch back to the larger trach size again to help prevent another blockage from forming. They had switched him to a smaller trach to see if that would make it easier for Bryan to talk. It was decided that the trach's inner cannula, or tube, would be changed every eight hours.

People asked me all the time why I stayed at the hospital twenty-four seven. This was why. Being forty-five minutes away, I felt helpless. Things could still change in a split second. One minute I was rubbing Bryan's legs; the next minute he was having a code blue. I wasn't going to let Bryan be alone through all the ups and downs. I needed him to know that I was there. Scary things are more scary when you go through them alone.

The same applied to me. I needed others to be there for me, and I had them. I couldn't have handled the code blue alone. Stewy and Shelly held me up and carried me through. I felt bad that Stewy had come all this way to see Bryan's eyes open, which they had been, but now Bryan was back on the ventilator. The extremes of emotions were staggering, from pure elation to devastation. We all needed each other to get through this.

The kids were supposed to come up to the hospital that afternoon. Sundays are our family day. The kids were in so many activities that this was the day we set aside for our time, but today it couldn't happen. I shakily dialed the number. "Mom, Bryan had a major setback," I sobbed.

"What happened?" she gasped.

"Bryan stopped breathing and now he is back on the ventilator," I barely managed to get out.

"Oh my God. That's terrible."

"I think it's best not to come today."

"That probably would be the best," my mom said.

"I'll call you later. I need to go."

"OK. I love you, Shauna. Stay strong, honey."

"Thanks, Mom. I love you, too."

It was difficult knowing I wouldn't see the kids, but I wasn't in the right mindset to see them. It was hard to see Bryan back on the vent and unresponsive. Just thinking how quickly things could go wrong rocked me to my core. I wish I could wrap myself up in a cocoon and be safe and protected from harm. Bryan's lab results came back pointing toward pneumonia. *Shit.*

By early evening, Bryan was off the vent, his fever was down, and he was sitting in his lounge chair, which his bed converted into with a press of a button. Bryan was oblivious to what had happened to him, for which I was thankful. It was as if he had taken a nap. With these turn of events, I called my parents back and told them to bring the kids up even if it was for a short time.

I was so happy to see the kids, especially after the last nine hours. I held on to Griffin and Elyse for an extra-long, tight hug. I didn't want to let go. Finally they said, "Mmmoooooommmmm."

Erica drove over from Chippewa Falls for a quick visit. She treated us to an Italian dinner from a local restaurant. It was nice to have my family, Stewy, and Shelly all together, laughing, talking, and having good food. It almost felt like things were back to normal.

Everyone took turns going back to visit with Bryan. When my parents came back, I knew it was almost time for the kids to leave.

It wasn't easy to get Griffin and Elyse to go back and see Bryan. I held their hands as we walked back to his room. We stood in our usual spot. Bryan was upright with his bed converted to a chair. The kids quickly waved and said, "Hi. I love you."

Bryan mouthed, "I love you, too."

"Bye, Dad," Griffin said.

"We will see you next week," Elyse said.

Bryan waved goodbye.

Then we turned to leave. Back down the hall we went. Goodbyes were said, and off they went. I prayed for the day when the kids would *want* to go and see Bryan without any coaxing.

Shelly, Stewy, and I went to Bryan's room. He tried to grab our hands and pull himself up as he mouthed the words, "Get me out of here."

"If I could, I would. Believe me, there is nothing more I want than to take you home," I told him.

After three short days, it was time for Stewy to go back to Texas. Even though he had to witness Bryan's code blue, Stewy got to see Bryan's eyes open and converse with him. As he left, he said, "Mission accomplished."

It was back to reality. Even though the doctors had closed the abdominal muscles, they had warned me that there was a possibility that they could come apart. If it did, they would not try to close it again. The abdominal skin was left open so the doctors could look directly at the muscles. It became a part of the doctor's daily routine to remove the dressings and check the abdominal stitches holding Bryan's muscles together. His abdomen stayed closed for fifteen days after the surgery, but then the muscles pulled apart. It was only a tiny opening, but it was enough to warrant yet another surgery to fix it. I was only shown his abdomen after it started to dehisce. It looked like when a shirt is too tight and the buttons are about to pop off. There are those little openings between each button. That was what was starting to happen to Bryan's abdomen.

"We need to do surgery right away. The muscles will be reopened, and a mesh will be sewn in to cover Bryan's remaining intestines for protection. He will have an abdominal hernia. Later, when the swelling in that area is down, we will do a skin graft to cover it. We will not try to close his abdominal muscles again. It is too risky. If the intestine were to come through a small opening and get twisted or pinched, it could cut off blood flow. That part of the intestine could die. Bryan only has just enough intestine to live. He can't lose anymore," said Dr. Farhat.

When I heard the word "hernia," I thought of my dad and sister. They both had hernias and it was no big deal. It was just a little bulge that would pop out when they sat or stood up. The bulge being the intestine coming out of a tear in the abdominal muscle, it was corrected with minor surgery.

But when the doctors showed me Bryan's hernia, I gasped. It was not just a little bulge but his whole lower abdomen. It looked like they forgot to close Bryan's abdomen after it was sliced open from the base of his sternum to his belt line. From the top to the bottom, it was ten inches long and seven inches at its widest point. It was the shape of a pear—narrow at the top and round at the bottom—covering the entire belly button area. The hernia opening needed to be that big to reduce the risk of the intestines being restricted, getting pinched or twisted, which could lead to obstructions. Obstructions could cause damage to the intestines and have to be surgically removed. This was not an option for Bryan. He couldn't live if he had any more of his intestines removed, so the abdominal hernia would be a permanent thing.

Dr. Farhat was a bit concerned about an area in Bryan's abdomen. He wanted to do a CT scan of that area to see if they needed to put in an additional drain to keep the area clean. *How can his abdomen still have an infected area?* Luckily, the CT scan came back clear.

The next morning, Bryan had to have another procedure. The doctors wanted to try the tube feedings again to get Bryan's GI system functioning and eventually become self-sufficient. Since the previous feeding tube in which the nutrients went directly into his stomach didn't work, the doctors wanted to try a G-J tube, a type of feeding tube that is put down through the stomach, bypassing it to deposit the nutrients directly into the small intestine. The G-J tube was inserted into the side of his abdomen. Along with the tube feedings, Bryan would continue to get TPN, since that was his only source of sustenance that was working. The more nutrition that could go through his digestive system, the better for keeping his GI tract active.

It seemed like there was rarely a day that Bryan didn't have to get some type of scan, procedure, X-ray, or surgery. *His poor body. How much more can it take?*

It didn't surprise me that Jenny, my college roommate and dear friend, designed a logo for our family: a male cyclist racing over the words "JOASSTRONG." Underneath was the motto: "Faith, Family, Friends." Jenny had asked me what Bryan's favorite color was; hence, the logo was red. She organized the JoasStrong apparel fundraiser six days after the accident. She worked with the Swag Shop, a local company, to get t-shirts, sweatshirts, and bumper stickers printed. Everything was sold online, with a portion of the sales being donated to our family.

She decided to make Wednesday, April 6, 2016, #JoasStrong Day. Jenny requested through Facebook, Instagram, Twitter, and CaringBridge:

> Please share this event with anyone who would be interested in showing their support for Bryan, Shauna, and their family by wearing #JoasStrong gear and/or red on Wednesday, April 6th. Remember to take pictures and post them on Facebook, Instagram, and/or Twitter using #JoasStrong. Thank you in advance for your support! Together, we are #JoasStrong!

My Facebook page was flooded with hundreds of pictures and words of encouragement. I couldn't believe people from our past and present, friends of friends, and strangers wearing OUR shirt. Many were making a heart with their hands or holding up homemade #JoasStrong signs. I chuckled when seeing the family pets, including Stewy's donkeys, wearing red collars, handkerchiefs, and even the JoasStrong shirt. Words accompanied many of the posts: "Stay strong," "You are in our prayers," "Keep fighting," "We love you," etc.

Every time I looked, there were more pictures and more words. Tears of amazement and gratitude ran down my face. I could feel the love jump out from the computer to soothe my soul. I wanted more than anything to share all the posts with Bryan, but that wasn't possible right now. He wasn't able to comprehend them. When the time was right, I would show him.

This JoasStrong Day couldn't have come at a better time. We had made it through thirty days of this hellish journey with no end in sight. Knowing we had so many holding us up reenergized me. I could make it through another day.

A couple of days later, my coworker, Betsy, emailed me. "You are never going to believe this," she wrote. "I met the young couple who were with Bryan at the accident scene. They ordered JoasStrong shirts. When I delivered the shirts, they explained to me who they were. They wondered if it would be alright for them to contact you. I hope you don't mind, but I told them 'of course,' that you would love to talk with them or even meet them."

"Oh my God. That is incredible. I would love to meet them," I responded.

She gave me their names, Alexa and Tony, along with Alexa's phone number. Before I even had a chance to call, Tony messaged me on CaringBridge:

> Shauna,
>
> My girlfriend Alexa and I were at Bryan's accident shortly after he was hit. We have been following his recovery since. We have a small gift basket we would like to drop off for you guys. We know that things are really busy for you and don't want to interrupt anything. We could meet at the hospital and give it to you, or wherever you see fit. Let us know!
>
> Thanks,
>
> Tony & Alexa

After a few text messages back and forth, a meeting was set up for them to come to the hospital. I couldn't wait to talk to them and give them a hug to thank them for taking such good care of Bryan when I couldn't.

Four days later, the day finally arrived when I would meet Bryan's angels. They wouldn't be coming until the evening, so I had the whole day to wait. It would have felt like an eternity waiting for them, but my day went by quickly because it was filled with many visitors.

Carmen and Jill brought me lunch. Some of our hockey friends, Mike and Kristin, hung out with me for the afternoon. As we were talking, Mike told me that he and another hockey dad, Grant, who has his pilot license, went up flying over the area of the accident. They were looking for the light-colored truck that was the suspected vehicle. They thought maybe they would find it hiding behind a barn or tucked away in a remote spot. Mike had forgotten how afraid of heights he was, but he and Grant were so hoping to find the truck, he powered through it. Unfortunately, nothing came from their mission, though I was grateful for the act of kindness.

Another workout partner, Kathy, and her husband, Bill, brought me dinner. Kathy and I had been workout partners since Bryan and I were dating. We started talking during our fitness classes at 5:30 a.m. Kathy worked in the same school district, and we became good friends. They were so gracious and made a point to bring dinner to me once a week. They always asked who was going to be there with me so they would be sure to have enough for everyone. This week's dinner was an incredible turkey dinner from McGovern's Pub in Saint Paul. It was like eating my dad's Thanksgiving dinner in April. Turkey, mashed potatoes, stuffing, corn, gravy—delicious!

As we were finishing up with dinner, Tony and Alexa peeked around the corner of the family lounge. "Shauna?"

They were here. They looked so young. Maybe in their mid-twenties. Alexa was small, thin, and shy. She had long brown hair and a beautiful, sweet smile. Tony was tall and outgoing. He had short brown hair that stuck up in front like Bryan's, with sideburns. He walked right in and introduced himself and Alexa.

I jumped up and ran to hug them. "Yes, it's me. Thank you for coming. I can't believe you're here. Come, sit down."

"Thanks for agreeing to see us," Tony said.

Alexa handed me a basket full of gifts. "This is for you and the kids."

There were snacks and passes to a local petting zoo. "Griffin and Elyse will love these. The petting zoo will be a fun outing."

Then I lifted out an embroidered wall hanging. "This is absolutely gorgeous," I exclaimed.

"I embroidered that a few days before Bryan's accident. The verse seems so appropriate now. I want you to have it," Alexa told me. "'Rejoice in hope. Be patient in tribulation. Be constant in prayer. Romans 12:12.'"

"You're right. The verse is so appropriate. No truer words could be spoken," I said. "It blows my mind that you made this before Bryan's accident. How could you have ever known what a comfort those words would be?"

"There's also some candy to give to the nurses," Alexa added. "Being a nurse, I know how much they will appreciate getting treats."

"How do I thank you two enough? You have already done so much for my family and now all of this? You are the definition of angels here on earth."

"We haven't stopped thinking about Bryan since the accident," said Tony.

"I have thought about you, also," I told them. "Since you were some of the first people at the accident scene, can you share with me what happened that day?"

Alexa and Tony sat down in chairs across from me. "We were on our way to the grocery store," Alexa began, "and saw cars stopped up ahead. I thought someone had hit a deer, so I told Tony to drive up there to make sure everything was OK."

"I wanted to turn down another road and just go to the grocery store, but Alexa insisted we go," Tony said.

"Thank God you did," I interjected.

"We soon discovered it was not a deer," Alexa continued, "but a bicyclist in the grass, teeth covered in dirt, helmet on, bike in the middle of the road and one wheel off somewhere else. The only visible bleeding came from a gash above his right knee. I could tell his pelvis was mangled. Luckily, he had his tight spandex bike shorts on to help keep it secure. I suspected from my medical background—I'm a NICU (neonatal intensive care) nurse—that with injuries like that, there would be internal bleeding, along with a possible spinal injury. I felt the best course of action was to stabilize his neck by putting his head between my knees."

"Oh, it was you," I interrupted. "I talked to a woman named Terry who was also at the scene. She told me about a nurse holding Bryan's head between her knees and instructing people what to do. It was you!"

"Yes, it was me," she continued. "At first, Bryan said, 'I'm OK,' and then soon after said, 'I need help.'"

"It is hard for me to believe that after being hit by a truck and so severely injured, that he was able to say a few words to you."

"But those were his only words. His helmet was still on but cockeyed. I knew I needed to unbuckle the strap to make sure his breathing wasn't restricted. Bryan immediately pushed the helmet off and wrapped his arm over his head."

"Oh my God. That arm thing is uncanny," I said, shaking my head. "Bryan puts his arm in that position often. I know it sounds weird, but he does that when he's watching TV, having a conversation, and lying in bed. It is very natural for him. Don't ask me why."

"Wow, that is crazy," Tony said. "As for me, I couldn't handle seeing Bryan, so I walked aimlessly around the accident scene. I happened to stumble upon a baggie that had a wallet and phone in it. The phone wasn't smashed. I tried to turn it on, but it wouldn't. I looked in the wallet to find the driver's license. I ran back to Alexa. 'Call him Bryan. His name is Bryan.'"

"While Tony was wandering around," Alexa said, "others came to help me. I asked if anyone had blankets, to go get them. One person suggested raising Bryan's legs, but I told them NO, absolutely not. We were going to wait for the ambulance to arrive. As we waited, a woman came to where we were and started praying over Bryan. When the ambulance got there, the medics began pushing on his abdomen. Bryan made moaning sounds. Upon quick examination, they determined that he was in dire need and had to be airlifted to a trauma hospital. Bryan was put into the ambulance while they waited for the helicopter to arrive. To us it seemed to take forever. The helicopter landed right on the road. They quickly transferred Bryan to the helicopter and away they flew."

"Wow. Even in all of this, Bryan was so lucky to have you and all the others taking care of him."

"We had to stay and get questioned by the police," Tony said. "They wanted to know if there were any suspicious vehicles. The only thing that seemed off was, when a white truck came by the scene, it wouldn't slow down even after someone, who was trying to direct traffic, told them to. That is where the initial report of a white truck came from."

"After we were finally done with the police questioning, we returned home. We couldn't sleep. We were haunted by what we had seen. We tried looking online for any updates but couldn't remember Bryan's last name. The next day, we saw an update on the news and started following your CaringBridge site," Alexa said. "We had to meet you."

"I am so glad you came. You were both such a crucial part of Bryan's survival."

We carried on a conversation about each other's jobs, a little about the kids, and life at the hospital.

"We don't want to keep you any longer. Thank you for letting us come," Tony said.

"No. Thank you. I have learned so much from the two of you. You will forever hold a special place in my heart." We hugged goodbye with the promise that, when Bryan was better, we would meet again.

"We would love that," they said.

As I lay on the loveseat bed that night, I couldn't help think of where we would be without Alexa and Tony. I truly believe that their being called to the scene was another miracle placed in Bryan's path. Alexa was a NICU nurse. In her quiet demeanor, she expertly took control of the situation. Holding Bryan's head in place and not allowing his legs to be moved, she prevented further injury and possible paralysis. Tony, in his own words, "freaked out," yet he got the blankets to keep Bryan warm and, wandering around the scene, found Bryan's vital information. They could call Bryan by his name to help calm him. More importantly, it allowed the police to get to me faster.

Chapter 15

I had done interviews with every TV news station in the Twin Cities at least once. Each interview got easier because talking from the heart about our story was a no-brainer. I wasn't nervous. Once the question was asked, the words just flowed. It also helped to know that, if I stumbled on something, it could easily be edited. What really gave me the strength to do this was the fact that the detectives on Bryan's case wanted this. They were trying to keep the story from being forgotten. There was not much evidence at the accident scene. It was their hope that someone from the public would see the broadcast and come forward with valuable information to solve the case.

After airing on TV, each news interview was posted on their websites. It was there that anyone could post comments. There were so many people wishing us well and praying for us. I would have never guessed there would be negative comments, but I was terribly wrong. I was winding down for the night, sitting on my "bed," wrapped in a blanket, and as usual, was checking CaringBridge and Facebook. There had been a news story earlier that night, so it was now posted online. Reading through the comments, one comment in particular haunted me . . . and still haunts me to this day: "Bikers shouldn't be on the road. If he dies, it's his fault." As I absorbed the words, I began to shake. My heart raced with anger and tears streamed down my cheeks. *How could someone be so cruel and heartless?*

Social media gives people the freedom to say whatever they want, without having to face that person. I knew that but still couldn't believe someone would say something like that. I immediately started pounding out a response on the keyboard. "This is my husband you're talking about. There are laws that give a biker every right to be on the roads. How dare you say it is his fault?" But something stopped me before I pressed send. Would I really change this person's belief? What do I tell my students to do if someone says something mean to them? Walk away. Take a deep breath. Count to ten. I couldn't waste my energy on this negativity, but it doesn't mean it didn't hurt. There were other negative comments, but none were as cruel as that one. After that, I stopped reading the comments on the interviews and just focused on the love and support from the CaringBridge comments.

As much as social media was a curse, it also was a blessing. As Bryan's status became more stable, I only needed to update CaringBridge once a day. It became a part of the evening routine. I would summarize the day's events, tell people specific prayer needs, and always finish with a "thank you." People would never know how much their responses refueled me and renewed my energy to get through another day.

Bryan was hardly sleeping. He continued to insist on being taken home. "Take me home. I want to go home," he would mouth. He would also point to the doorway. It was clear being at the hospital and being taken care of by a team of doctors was not restful for him.

"Bryan, you were in a bad accident. Someone hit you when you were riding your bike. When your body is ready, we can go home. This is where you need to be for recovery," I would explain to him. He would nod in understanding and then doze off.

When he would wake up, he would ask me the same questions again. I started to realize that Bryan may not fully understand or comprehend what had happened to him. It reminded me of someone coming out of anesthesia. They are awake and listening to the doctor and then fall back asleep, wake up, and ask if the doctor has come in yet. This was happening to Bryan on repeat for about two weeks. *Is this really how long it takes to wake up from a coma? He seemed awake, but is he really?*

As the days turned into weeks, I began to worry about Bryan's mental health. I had heard about PTSD or depression in similar traumatic situations. It could be debilitating if not treated. If he was dealing with any symptoms, I wanted to be proactive and stop it before it spiraled out of control.

Bryan hadn't been showing any outward signs of depression, but it didn't stop me from wondering how someone could not be depressed going through an ordeal like that. His life had been completely turned upside down. He had gone from being a strong, active, healthy person to someone who was confined to a bed. He would get exhausted trying to lift a one-pound weight or trying to talk. I could see the total frustration in his eyes. Therefore, I knew I needed to bring my concern to his care team.

The ICU doctors and nurses were so focused on Bryan's physical needs that they weren't concerned about his mental needs. I brought the worry of depression up at one of the daily conference meetings. The doctors understood my concerns and assigned a psychologist to come and talk to Bran at least once a week. I was grateful to have another set of eyes and ears looking and listening to Bryan in a different light. I wanted to make sure I wasn't missing a key component to Bryan's recovery.

The nurses weren't too concerned with Bryan's lack of sleep. They thought he might have his days and nights mixed up, which was very common in the ICU. The ICU was an active area, with lots of movement. The lights were dimmed but never fully off. The nurses were in at least every two hours, rolling Bryan from side to side and checking his vitals. This made for disruptive sleep, if he had fallen asleep. So like when Elyse was a baby and her days and nights were flipped, we tried to keep Bryan awake during the day and not let him take any naps. We also had him do his exercises a few extra times to try and tire him out. I began putting lavender oil in the diffuser at night. Lavender was commonly used for restlessness, insomnia, and depression. I was willing to try anything. Unfortunately, nothing seemed to work. He continued to have sleepless nights. Every morning, the nurse would report that Bryan was up for most of the night. I didn't know what else to do.

Nurse Kay got Bryan a room change. It was another attempt in trying to boost his spirits. Bryan's new room had a window that looked out to the park behind the hospital. Even though Bryan's bed was facing away from the window, there was lots of natural light coming in. We turned his bed a few times, but Bryan didn't really seem to care. He didn't even try to look out the window. He would just lie in the same position with a blank look on his face. He really didn't seem interested in anything, which was concerning. I was glad the psychologist was now part of his care team.

The doctors continued with the tube feedings directly into Bryan's intestines. After they let the stomach rest for five days, they wanted to try to put nutrients directly into his stomach again to determine if it would begin to work. The nurses started the feeding tube at a slow drip, but almost as soon as they would put the nutrients in, it would come gushing out into his ileostomy bag. Not much absorption could happen with how quickly it was going through him, but it was a positive sign that Bryan's stomach and what was left of his small intestine were pushing the nutrients through the system. They needed to get things to slow down; therefore, they adjusted the medications Bryan was already getting, in hopes that it would help. *Will his GI system ever absorb enough nutrients for him to not have to do TPN, or will TPN become a permanent need?* I wasn't told how long Bryan could be on TPN or if it was something that he could do indefinitely. I guess it would be something we'd figure out as we went along on the journey.

Bryan's white blood count continued to be elevated. When the white blood count is elevated, it means the body is trying to fight an infection. A normal white blood count is between four thousand and eleven thousand. Anything over ten thousand five hundred is considered high. Bryan's was thirty-one thousand. He didn't have a fever, but the doctors were very concerned about that number. Dr. Farhat called in the infectious disease specialist. They did a CT scan of his chest, abdomen, and pelvis to see if they could locate the source of infection causing the high white blood count. No source found. The worry of infections came flooding back. "It wasn't the cancer; it was the infection that killed them." "It wasn't the surgery; it was the infection." I was petrified. *How could his white blood count be so high and there be no source? If they can't find a source, how can they treat Bryan accurately? Am I going to lose Bryan to an infection after all he's survived?*

The doctors decided to continue to keep Bryan on a general antibiotic and hoped that would do the trick. It was all they could do. I prayed it would be enough.

The nurses knew I was staying overnight in the lounge, so when Bryan would get anxious and ask for me, they weren't hesitant to come get me. Today, they woke me at 4:00 a.m. It happened to be our eleventh wedding anniversary, so for an instant I thought maybe he wanted to wish me a happy anniversary, but I knew that wasn't it.

As soon as I stepped into the room, I could see Bryan's stress ease immediately. The constant fidgeting and restlessness of his body subsided. With a big exhalation, he seemed to melt into the bed. "Good morning, honey," I whispered as I began rubbing his feet. Bryan closed his eyes while his breathing became more even. Mike, who was a physical therapist, had taught me how to rub his feet in order to work out the fluid that had built up from his immobility. Slowly, I worked my way up his legs. I stayed the rest of the early morning, sitting on the folding chair with my head resting on his bed, gently rubbing his legs until I fell asleep. But sleep never lasted long. I would wake to Bryan moving his arm or leg, his gentle way of telling me to keep rubbing.

I couldn't help think about our wedding day eleven years ago. I had woken up early, anxious and excited to be getting married. It was a beautiful April day. The sun was shining, and it was seventy-five degrees, not the norm in Minnesota for April. Our wedding was small, simple, and perfect. I had gotten my wedding dress at Bloomingdale's for one hundred thirty-five dollars in the prom section. It was a strapless, A-lined, champagne-colored dress with subtle embroidered vine and flowers covering the whole dress. Bryan wore a brown-toned suit with a champagne-colored shirt to coordinate with my dress. Erica was my matron of honor, and Stewy was Bryan's best man.

Our wedding was officiated by one of my friends, Stacie. She told us, "Even though you are uniting as one today, you still need to develop your own special gifts as individuals. There are going to be detours, pit stops, and times when you need to slow down on your journey, but together you will get through it." Neither of us could have predicted the ways we would be tested. Neither of us could have imagined what we were living through now.

We didn't have a wedding cake. Bryan likes cookies and I like ice cream, so we had sugar cookies with buttercream frosting made at Cub Foods; and the owner of our hometown creamery, Olson's, made us our very own ice cream, Butterfinger and peanut butter cups. They put them into individual cups for us. A special touch to make our wedding unique.

Sitting here in the ICU eleven years later, instead of the blushing bride, I was the nurturing mother. It almost seemed like I was reliving those long, long nights trying to get baby Elyse to sleep and stay asleep. Rocking her back and forth in the chair was like rubbing Bryan's legs. I did it until I could hardly keep my eyes open. When I thought she was finally asleep, I would slowly get up from the chair, being careful not to move her. As I laid her back in her crib, I prayed that, when I slid my hand out from under her, she wouldn't wake up. But there were many nights I would only get to the doorway before she started crying again. I resorted to sleeping on the floor next to her with my hand resting on her back. Now I slept in a folding chair with my hand on Bryan. They both needed to know someone who loved them was there.

Almost two years ago, on my thirty-ninth birthday, Bryan surprised me with a Rick Steves book about Italy. Inside there was a note saying, "This is where YOU AND I are going to celebrate our tenth anniversary." I had heard that Italy was one of the most romantic places, and now we were going there. After my initial shock, I put my arms around him and said, "Bryan, I can't believe you did this. I love you so much. We are going to have the best time ever."

This was the first time we had been away from the kids, so I was apprehensive. But my parents agreed to take care of the kids. They would come to Eagan for four days and take the kids to school and their activities. Then over spring break, they would take them to Chippewa Falls. The kids were excited to spend time with Aunt Erica and Morgan and Ingrid, as well as Grandpa and Grandma Joas.

There was so much preplanning for a trip like this. It wasn't just the packing, the passports, booking reservations, etc., but the realization that we were going to be so far away. It really hit home when we wrote a will. Even though I had flown many times, this was the first time I was crossing the ocean to a foreign country. *What if something happens to us?*

But once Bryan and I got on the plane, my worries vanished. Our itinerary was full as we wanted to take in everything. We started our whirlwind adventure with five days in Rome. We walked many miles every day, trying to see as many of the historical sites as we could: the Colosseum, the Pantheon, and the Sistine Chapel were just a few of the incredible sights we saw. While waiting to tour Saint Peter's Basilica, we looked up and saw Pope Francis getting ready to hold his Papal Audience. Even though neither of us are Catholic, it was an honor to receive his blessing.

The next leg of the trip was a train ride to Florence. We received another blessing by rubbing the nose of Porcellino, the Bronze Hog, who, according to legend, brings good luck. We walked across the Ponte Vecchio Bridge and toured all the museums, with the highlight of seeing the statue of David.

The final leg of our trip was Venice. Even though it rained the whole time we were there, we walked along the canals and enjoyed the beauty of the "Floating City." We saw t-shirts about how the rats come out at night, so naturally, I made Bryan go on a rat hunt with me. After just a few turns, we could attest to the rats in Venice, scurrying near the garbage cans. Even with the witnessing of the rats, the magic of Venice wasn't dimmed.

It was a glorious twelve days of reconnecting with each other along with marveling at the scenic beauty, the museums, the art, and the architecture. We found ourselves saying over and over again, "This is amazing. I can't believe these were built over two thousand years ago." We savored Italian cuisine and wine in quaint cafes and candle-lit fine restaurants, always toasting our ten years of marriage. Now, a year later, I sat at the side of Bryan's hospital bed, rubbing his atrophied legs, wondering if we'd ever be able to take another trip like that. I couldn't help but let the tears flow.

Chapter 16

It was Sunday, thirty-four days after the accident, and the kids and I were in the hospital lounge. When I asked if either one wanted to go back and see their dad, Elyse surprised me by saying, "I do." Griffin shook his head no.

I reminded her that talking with her dad was a little different than it used to be. "He can mouth words, but no sound will come out. He can use his hands to give you a thumbs up or thumbs down. He will nod his head yes and no. You can talk to him and tell him about school or friends. He wants to know what is happening with you both."

Elyse nodded, and I took her hand and we headed back to Bryan's room. At the threshold of his room, where we usually stopped and went no further, she let go of my hand and continued to walk right into his room and up to his bed. She took his hand in hers. I stood frozen in disbelief. I saw Bryan smile and mouth the words, "I love you."

"I love you too, Dad," Elyse said, and my heart burst with pure joy.

I joined Elyse at Bryan's bedside and put my arm around her. There was nothing I could say. I leaned over and kissed the top of her head and whispered, "Oh Elyse, thank you."

Then she turned and asked, "Can we go now?"

"Say goodbye to Dad," I told her.

"Bye," she said to him as she waved and left the room.

"I'll be back in a bit," I told him.

As we walked down the hall, I thought to myself, *Elyse, you don't know what a huge step that was.* I hoped this would be the start of the new normal.

Griffin took a LOT more convincing. At first this really bothered me. Bryan and Griffin were so close; they were best buddies. Bryan was his coach for football, hockey, lacrosse, and even soccer. Griffin looked up to him. Yet, he didn't want to go back and see him. I just couldn't understand. Then my mom told me that almost every night Griffin would say, "My dad is never going to be the same. He's never going to coach me. He'll never play outside with me. Everything has changed." It was then I could see why Griffin was reluctant to go see Bryan. He was terrified. I had thought he was scared of the hospital, the machines, or how Bryan looked. But it was that he thought he'd lost the dad he knew and loved.

The next time my parents brought the kids to the hospital, I pulled Griffin into the hall and sat down with him.

"Griffin, I know you are scared your dad isn't going to ever be the same. But your dad has come so far and the doctors feel that he will someday be well. It isn't easy. It takes time."

He looked at me with big tears in his eyes, blinking those long eyelashes and shaking his head.

"Right now, it's our turn to be the coaches. We need to give Dad encouragement and hope. He loves you and Elyse more than anything. You both are why he is fighting so hard. You need to let him know you are with him."

Griffin started crying, and I gave him a hug. My poor, dear boy.

"I need you to go down and say hi. I will be with you."

"I'm so scared."

"I know, honey. You are being so brave. I am proud of you. Dad is, too. You can do this."

I convinced him to go back to Bryan's room. I promised him we would stand outside. Mike and Gregg were already in the room visiting with Bryan. There was a recliner chair outside the room, so Griffin and I sat there. Griffin just quietly watched. The guys were joking, laughing, and telling stories from their biking escapades.

"Bryan, when you get out of here, we are going to go back and ride the Tail of the Dragon," Mike said.

"Yeah. We drove all the way to North Carolina to ride it, only to be stopped at the entrance by the state trooper, gun and all, sitting in a lawn chair, to tell us the road was closed," Gregg retorted. "Those damn landslides."

"Epic fail," Mike replied. "But we totally could have hiked over them."

Bryan shook his head.

"We will ride the Tail of the Dragon," Mike continued, "even if I have to strap you to my back."

"OK, princess," Gregg said, "I would love to see that."

Bryan smiled and laughed.

Seeing the guys bantering back and forth made it almost seem normal, but I missed hearing Bryan's smartass comments back to Mike and Gregg. "Princess" was a nickname given to Mike because Bryan and Gregg would want to drive through the night, but Mike would need his beauty sleep. He couldn't sleep in cars. I knew Bryan's comebacks would come as soon as he started talking again.

I saw a smile appear on Griffin's face as he watched the scene. It was as if the fear was starting to fade. To my surprise, Griffin stood up and stepped into the room without saying a word. He slowly walked over and crawled into Mike's lap, becoming more a part of the conversation. He laughed at their jokes and talked a bit.

After a while, I said, "Griffin, it's almost time for you to go home. You have school tomorrow."

Without any prompting, Griffin went over to Bryan and took his hand. "I love you, Dad."

"I love you, too, buddy," Bryan mouthed back.

There weren't any dry eyes in the room.

"Way to go, Sally," Mike said to Griffin, giving him a high five. Sally was a silly nickname Mike gave to Griffin.

"See ya, buddy," Gregg said to Griffin, giving him a fist bump.

As Griffin left the room, he had a smile from ear to ear. What a huge hurdle he'd just leaped.

Walking back to the lounge, I put my arm around his shoulder. "Griffin, I am so proud of you. Just think how happy you made your dad. Now it will be so much easier the next time you come. You should be proud of yourself, too."

"Yeah," he replied leaning in and giving me a hug.

After my mom and dad took the kids home, I sat in the lounge by myself. I closed my eyes and took a deep breath. Griffin and Elyse both had taken giant steps forward in their healing process without any prodding. They each did it on their own terms. They weren't afraid of their dad any more. My prayers were answered, and a sense of gratitude and relief washed over me.

Chapter 17

The next day when the speech therapist came in, she told me, "I'm switching Bryan's trach tube to a smaller one. We need to get him talking. Hopefully this will make it easier."

It would be such a relief to hear Bryan's voice again. He had been trying but just couldn't produce any sounds. So for thirty-five days, I hadn't heard his voice. I was getting better at understanding what he was telling me. But when I couldn't figure it out, he would get frustrated. He would shake his head no, roll his eyes, and mouth "whatever." Then he would shut down and not try again, sort of like a teenager.

After the new trach was put in, the Passy-Muir valve went on the end of the tube that stuck out of Bryan's throat. The valve only went on for eating, drinking, or talking. The therapist started with having Bryan hum. It was a lot of work for him to get the air to go all the way up through his vocal chords, but he did it. Then the next step.

"Say hi," the therapist said.

I held my breath. *Please, please let this happen.*

He took a deep breath in. Then, in a raspy whisper, Bryan said, "Hi."

Did I really hear that? Yes! He really did it. That little two-letter word never sounded more glorious. "Hi," I stammered back.

It was astonishing how much work it took for Bryan to say that one little word. He was exhausted but not enough to stop smiling. The therapist tried to ask a few more questions, which he struggled to answer. He didn't have the energy to force the sounds out.

"You've done a good job, Bryan. I'd like to have you try a swallow test," she said. "This will determine if you can start drinking or eating. I think you're ready. I will evaluate how you swallow and make sure nothing goes into your lungs. I need to go gather the supplies I need."

She was gone for fifteen minutes, which gave Bryan some time to rest. Even if Bryan could drink a bit of water, that would be huge. His mouth was always so dry that he would beg for something to drink or to chew on ice. It was getting harder to say no to him, especially with how persistent he was. It was very much like when the kids wanted something at Target and would beg relentlessly until I gave in.

The first test was to take a sip of water. I watched him nervously and hoped that I wouldn't hear the choking cough. He put his lips around the straw, sucked up the water, and swallowed.

Nothing. Beautiful silence. He passed that test. I quietly did a little happy dance.

Next up, applesauce. If he could swallow that without trouble, he would get clearance to start eating soft foods.

Boom. He passed that too.

"Let's stop there for today. You've had a big day, Bryan. Nice work," the therapist told him.

Bryan smiled, exhausted but elated.

She turned to me, "It's been thirty-five days since he has had anything orally, so I don't want to rush it."

"I understand. Thank you."

Now that Bryan knew he could drink, the first thing he asked for was a root beer float. I found that an odd request because I couldn't remember him ever having one before. But if a root beer float was what he wanted, then we'd figure out how to get him one. Later I would understand his desire for a root beer float.

Before he went to bed, I said to him, "You have to call the kids and say something."

He shook his head no.

"Why? Just say hi so they can hear your voice. They need this, Bryan. Please."

He finally relented, and I called and spoke to Griffin first. "I have a surprise for you. Go get Elyse."

"OK, Mom." Then he yelled, "Elyse, Mom wants you to come here."

Bryan shakily put on the valve as I handed him the phone. "Hi. I love you," he whispered and then quickly handed me back the phone.

"Griffin, that was Dad. He can talk now, but it is really hard for him and makes him really tired. Can you put Elyse on so Dad can talk to her?"

"OK. That was so cool!" I could hear the excitement over the phone.

"I know."

I handed the phone back to Bryan. "Talk to Elyse."

"Hi, I love you." He threw the phone at me and ripped off the valve. Closing his eyes, he took many gasping deep breaths.

"Hi, Elyse. That was Dad. It is really hard for him to talk, but did you hear him?"

"Yeah."

"He can talk now. I wanted you to hear his voice."

"That didn't sound like him."

"I know. He has to put a special cover over the tube in his throat. It's going to sound a bit different for a while," I said, trying to reassure her. "I'll call you again tomorrow. I need to go. I love you."

"Bye. Love you, too. Tell Dad I love him."

When I called my mom the next day, the first thing she said was, "The kids couldn't stop talking about hearing their dad's voice. They were running around saying, 'I can't wait to tell my friends at school tomorrow.' Shauna, I wish I could have captured that moment for you. Those four words 'Hi, I love you.' Wow, wow, wow."

After hearing how much that phone call meant to Griffin and Elyse, I knew I had done the right thing by insisting that Bryan talk to them. I couldn't wait to relay my mom's message to him about how excited the kids were. He needed to know that his extra effort was worth it.

Chapter 18

After Griffin's birthday party, I posted a few of the pictures of the Gopher lacrosse players with him on Facebook. One of my former students, Elise, contacted me. She told me that Nick, her brother and also one of my former students, was on the team. She was also friends with all the players that had come to our house.

Elise was whom we named our Elyse after. She was one of my favorites. When I taught her in first grade, she was a cute little blondie, who was so sweet and polite, with a squeaky voice. She was a hard worker and good friend, everything you would want your own child to be.

Any teacher will tell you that it's difficult to decide on names for your own children. You associate most names with someone else. The longer you teach, the more names get taken off the list. Elise was the one girls' name that Bryan and I agreed on. We decided to spell it with a "y" because Bryan is spelled with a "y" instead of the typical "i."

After my students leave elementary school, I lose track of them. I remember running into Elise and her mom at Kohl's one day with my Elyse, who was about four at the time. It had been six years since I had seen them.

"Elise, this is my daughter Elyse." I turned to Elyse and said, "This is whom you are named after."

My dad and I thought it would be cool to take Griffin to a Gopher lacrosse game to see all the players that had come to the house. They were celebrities in Griffin's eyes. We finally decided the April 13 game would work. It was their last home game and Shani was available to stay with Bryan, so everything was covered. I contacted Elise through Facebook and wrote, "I was hoping you could let Nick and your friends know that my dad and I are planning on bringing Griffin to their lacrosse game on Wednesday night. Griffin is pretty excited to watch them play."

She wrote back, "Hi! I will definitely let them know! I'm glad he will be able to go watch them at their last home game this season. Nick said he was going to talk to his coach about letting Griffin sit on the sidelines with the team, so I will let you know if they are able to work that out!"

How cool would that be? Griffin would be in heaven.

She contacted me two days later and told me that Griffin would be their honorary captain for the game. "He will be on the field during warm-ups with them and go out with the other captains for the coin toss before the game," she wrote. "They will make sure to get him some Gopher gear to wear as well! He can then hang out on the sidelines with the boys for the remainder of the game. Nick said to try to have Griffin there around 7:15 p.m. so he can meet some of the guys a little before warm-ups!"

This was going to be so amazing! I didn't tell Griffin what would be happening. He just thought he was going to the game to watch them play and maybe get a chance to say hi after the game. I couldn't wait to see his reaction.

When we got to the stadium, Nick immediately came over to greet us. "Hi, Mrs. Joas and Griffin. Thanks for coming to the game. Griff, come with me. We are going to go on the field to warm up."

Nick looked the same as he did when he was six, just an older version: short with blonde hair and a kind smile. Griffin looked at me with a huge smile and wide eyes before following Nick on to the field where he helped pass the ball to the players as they ran their warm-up drills. I could see Griffin's smile from the stands.

This game happened to also be the Chris Jenkins's Memorial Invitational. It was a game honoring the life and memory of a former Gopher member and goalie of the team, Chris Jenkins, who had been a senior captain in 2001 when he disappeared on Halloween night. Following months of searching, Chris's body was found in the Mississippi River after it thawed in the spring.

Before the game, both teams gathered as Chris's parents talked to them about carrying on Chris's love for the game. Both teams presented Griffin with shorts and a team pinnie. Chris's parents gave us a book they wrote about their journey. His mom, Jan, told me, "Take your courage and keep moving forward. We hope for the best outcome for you." The Jenkins' family had a different outcome than us. But going through a trauma connected us. I was overcome with emotion and didn't have any words to answer her back. I could only just nod my head and mouth "Thank you."

Griffin was on the sidelines with the team for the whole game. They treated him like royalty. The Gopher lacrosse team went over and above to give him an extraordinary experience that he would never forget.

The game was over late, really late. I felt bad that I was gone so long. I called Shani to say, "When I drop everyone off, I'm going to take a quick shower and then come back to the hospital."

"No, Shauna. I got this. You sleep at home. I will see you in the morning."

"Are you sure?"

"Absolutely."

"Thank you," I said with relief.

I felt guilty for not going back to the hospital, but in reality, I wouldn't have gotten back until at least 11:30 p.m. and I knew Shani would be on top of things and would call if anything happened. I slept at HOME in my own bed . . . It was the first time in thirty-seven days. *Would I actually be able to sleep?*

The kids were excited to have me at home. We went to bed right away since it was a school night and already 10:30 p.m. Elyse and Griffin quickly got their pajamas on and jumped into bed with me.

"I will have to get up early and get back to the hospital before Shani has to go to work," I told them as we lay there.

"We know," they both answered.

"It is nice to have you here tonight," Griffin whispered, snuggling in a little more.

"It sure is nice to be here with you both, too."

"Good night, Mom," Elyse said.

"Good night. I love you both and am so proud of you."

They fell asleep quickly. They were the reason I had to keep moving forward. After a kiss on their foreheads, I fell asleep, too. Holding my babies close to me made for a perfect night's sleep.

Chapter 19

Bryan had been in the ICU for five weeks. He continued to make progress with no major setbacks for several days, and the doctors were pleased with him becoming more stable. At Bryan's daily medical meeting, Dr. Beal brought up the possibility of him being transferred out of the ICU and onto the main trauma floor within a few days.

And then Dr. Beal turned to the nurses. "It is such a beautiful day," he said. "Do you think it would be possible to give Bryan a change of scenery by wheeling him outside?"

"I think we could definitely do that," Nurse Eric said.

Dr. Beal said, "Let's go for it." The others at the meeting nodded in agreement.

As the nurses got things prepared for the great adventure outdoors, the respiratory therapist brought in the long-awaited root beer float. I was expecting Bryan to be more exuberant about it. Unfortunately, he took one sip and put it to the side where it sat until it melted and needed to be thrown out. For all the hype, it was a big letdown. Later I found out that with all actions to prepare to go outside, Bryan had anxiety from thinking about moving to the mobile bed. That anxiety overshadowed the delivery of the root beer float.

The nurses, Eric and Barb, transferred Bryan to a smaller hospital bed since the ICU bed wouldn't fit in the elevator or maneuver the hallways. They put a special cover over his trach. Catherine arrived just as we were leaving Bryan's room so she joined us. Then we were off, winding through the floors of the hospital, down the elevator, out the door, and up a long ramp to our final destination, which was a garden area on the side of the hospital. We laughed, as it looked like we were stealing someone from the hospital. Patients that are wheeled outside are usually in a wheelchair. Catherine took off her sunglasses and put them on Bryan so he wouldn't be blinded by the sun. Bryan didn't speak but just lay there with his eyes closed, feeling the sun on his face. Catherine and I made small talk with the nurses who were happy with their assignment.

The wind picked up, making it difficult for Bryan to breathe, so we went back inside. We only spent a mere thirty minutes outside, but those thirty minutes of sunshine and fresh air and doing something "normal" were a rejuvenation for both Bryan and me. Plus, we made history at North Memorial Hospital. This was the first time an ICU patient had ever been taken outside. Bryan kept it hidden that this event was not all that enjoyable for him and was uncomfortable. It was another step in the rehab process.

My in-laws, Steve and Jan, came to visit for the day every week or two. Every time I knew they were going to come, I would work myself into a tizzy because the same thing happened every time they came. Jan would sit for a few minutes and then want to go sit in the car. Steve would try to explain to her how to get to the parking ramp. "You go down the elevator to the first floor, walk all the way down the hall, past the front door all the way until you can't go any further. Take the elevator up to the fourth level in the parking ramp, and find the car. It should be to your left." After trying to explain it to her three or four times, she still seemed confused. You could tell he was frustrated and wasn't going to take her to the car. It was at that point Shani or another angel friend would come to the rescue and said, "Don't worry. I'll walk you to your car, Jan." Once in the car, she would stay there for up to three or four hours.

I didn't have the energy to take care of Jan. Inevitably, the conversation would always turn to how Steve could take away her driving privileges. Jan's cognitive skills had significantly declined, and it wasn't safe for her to be driving anymore. My friends and I gave Steve a plethora of ideas of how he could do it: hide the keys, have the doctor tell her, put her car at his brother's house, and so on. He would nod his head yes and say, "That's a good idea." But in reality, he did nothing. He didn't want to take away her last bit of independence. It was always a huge relief when they left. This scene repeated itself every time they came to visit.

Bryan was trying to eat now that he had passed the swallow test, but he would eat one or two bites and that was it. TPN is hard on the liver, which was already not working one hundred percent due to the trauma, so the doctors wanted him to eat more. The more he could physically eat and get the food to go through his digestive system, the less negative effect the TPN would have on his body. So every day we would try again. I would try to encourage him to eat even one more bite, but he refused. I could see now where Elyse got her stubbornness, but I was frustrated. *Didn't he know how important it is for him to actually eat? Is he even trying?* I guess I had to resign myself to the fact that, like everything else, this was going to be a SLOW process, too.

Later Bryan would explain to me why he couldn't eat. "You know when you are so full, that if you eat one more bite, you will throw up? That's how it felt all the time. Even thinking about food made me feel sick."

Bryan began to ask more questions when it was just the two of us sitting in his room. "Who hit me?"

"We think it was a truck but don't really know because the person didn't stop," I would explain.

"How did you find out?"

"The police came to the door. Griffin saw them first, and he came and got me."

Bryan just closed his eyes and shook his head. It was a lot to process.

"It's OK, honey. You are alive. We will figure things out," I said, trying to reassure him.

Then there would be nothing said about it until the next time he would bring it up. When he was ready, we would go through what happened. It had to be on his time.

Each time the speech therapist would come in, she would always ask Bryan, "Where are you?" "What is the name of the hospital?" "Where is the hospital located?" She was trying to determine if Bryan could create new memories. He finally could remember the name of the hospital. I couldn't blame him for not remembering it. I had a hard time remembering at first and had to ask people, "Where am I again?" North Memorial was not a hospital near us, so it was not in our vocabulary.

One morning when Erica was up visiting, the speech therapist came to do her session. Erica and I stayed in the room. When she asked Bryan where the hospital was located, he answered, "In my backyard."

Erica and I giggled. The speech therapist flashed us a dirty look. Bryan's humor was starting to show up. He was typically a quiet guy but had a quick wit. No one expected the hilarious one liners to come from him. Then she asked Bryan to name three things that fly. He answered, "Squirrels, magical reindeer, and—" Erica and I laughed out loud. I was so relieved to see that spark of humor.

The speech therapist cut Bryan off. "You need to take this seriously." She glared at us once again. She was not amused. She didn't stay long after that. I know she didn't appreciate Bryan's humor, but Erica and I sure did. To me, it was another sign Bryan's brain was not affected by his accident. It was almost him saying, "If you ask dumb questions, I am going to give you dumb answers." That was definitely the Bryan I knew.

I needed to go to the bathroom, so I left Erica with Bryan. As I was turning to go to the bathroom down the hall, I saw the nurse manager wheeling an empty cart into the ICU family lounge. I had seen her during my time in the ICU, usually sitting in her office. We had never spoken, and I had never seen her in the lounge area. I hesitated and thought, *What is she doing?*

I went to the bathroom and then made my way back to the lounge to check it out. Something about her going in there just didn't feel right to me.

When I walked into the lounge, my home for over five weeks, the nurse manager was loading all my things onto the cart. There on the cart is my pillow, toiletry bag, duffle bag, snacks, water, and the few cards and decorations we had on the windowsill. Tears of rage filled my eyes. I was shaking all over. Without hesitation, I frantically started ripping all my things off the cart and throwing them onto the floor.

"You can't be staying here," she scolded. "It isn't sanitary. There is a room across the street you can rent for only fifty dollars a day."

I could barely talk. My heart was racing. My face flushed with anger. *Fifty dollars a day. You have got to be kidding me? I don't know what Bryan's bills are going to be. We could go bankrupt because of this accident. I can't spend fifty dollars a day. I don't know how long he will be in the hospital.*

Finally I managed to stammer, "I have been here for over five weeks and you are just telling me this now?"

"Where did you get these sheets and blankets?" she asked accusingly.

"The nurses gave them to us," I retorted.

"I can help you take your things somewhere else," she told me.

"I don't need your help. I'll take care of it myself," I snapped and turned my back to her.

She wheeled her now empty cart away.

I dropped to the couch and cried so hard I was gasping and hiccupping. I had tried to do everything right, followed the rules, and not be in the way. I hate confrontation. This was humiliating. There were no rules for the lounge posted on the walls. No one from the ICU told me I was doing something wrong. They all knew we were staying there. This came out of the blue and felt like a kick in the gut.

The family that had been holding vigil for less than forty-eight hours in the middle section of the lounge came over to say they were sorry. They had been yelled at, too.

Erica came to find out what was taking so long and saw me crying. "What the hell happened?"

I tried to tell her what happened. "I have to take this to the car. Let's get out of here and I will tell you on the way," I said as I started grabbing my things.

After I calmed down, I told the nurses what had happened. They felt so bad. "You can stay in Bryan's room. We'll get you a recliner to sleep on."

"Thank you."

Thank God Bryan only had a couple of days left in the ICU.

The next day, I went back to the lounge to take a break from sitting in Bryan's room. I wanted to check on the family I had met in the lounge and thank them for helping me when I was getting yelled at by the nurse. We sat around the lounge table and shared our stories. Janelle's son, who was seventeen, was "car surfing" and he fell and cracked his skull resulting in a traumatic brain injury. He was in very critical condition. Part of his skull had to be removed because of the swelling in his brain. They were experiencing those "touch and go" situations that I had gone through.

When I went to dinner that night in the cafeteria by myself, I remembered the necklace that Carmen gave me. She had given me a Giving Key necklace at the start of our journey that said "HOPE." The "HOPE" necklace was something you were supposed to wear during your time of need, to offer you strength and encouragement. Then you are supposed to pay it forward by giving the necklace to someone who needs it more than you.

I had been wearing the necklace every day without a thought about who to give the necklace to. I was so wrapped up in our situation that it never crossed my mind that someone would need it more than I did. But at that moment, I knew I needed to pass it on to Janelle. Her family was just starting their very long journey. Bryan still had a long way to go, but he was out of the critical stage and getting ready to move out of the ICU.

I finished up my dinner and went straight to the lounge where I tapped Janelle on the shoulder. "Hi Janelle, my neighbor gave me this necklace," I said, showing her the necklace. "It is called a Giving Key necklace. You are supposed to wear the necklace for as long as you need it. When you find someone who needs it more than you, you pass it on."

I took the necklace and placed it around her neck.

"It worked for us, and now it will work for you."

"Thank you, Shauna. I won't take it off," Janelle said with her voice cracking, as we embraced.

Chapter 20

Since Bryan's accident, we had been getting packets in the mail from law firms around the area, but they all went directly into the garbage. Who would we sue? We didn't even know who did this to Bryan.

I was beginning to start thinking about how much this was all going to cost. The only bill we had received so far was fourteen thousand dollars for the helicopter ride. That was merely the ride. I knew that every time a nurse or a doctor came into the room, to even scan a tube, an IV bag, a bandage, etc., that we were being charged. *What would happen to our family? Would we be paying medical bills for the rest of our lives? Would we ever get to go on vacation again? Would we have to sell our house? Would life as we knew it be gone?*

As those questions began filling my daily thoughts, Dave, a high school classmate of Erica and Bryan, contacted Erica. He is a lawyer and wanted to pass along some advice: "The insurance companies don't want to pay out what you are entitled to. Tell Shauna not to settle."

What does that mean? What are we entitled to?

Ironically, the next day I got an email from an acquaintance of ours, Adam. His son played hockey and lacrosse with Griffin. He is an attorney, specializing in personal injury. He wrote, "I want to make sure you understand that Bryan is entitled to compensation through your car insurance regardless of whether or not the wrongdoer is identified and caught for what he/she did. Insurance companies often do not inform people of their full rights under the policy in situations like this."

I was getting the same advice from two people who were looking out for our best interests. It was reassuring that I wouldn't be taken advantage of and the legal aspects would be covered. Therefore, I contacted Adam to set up an appointment.

Adam came the morning of Bryan's moving day out of the ICU. He was a short, stocky guy with short brown spiked hair. He was dressed in a suit and tie, shiny black shoes, a briefcase at his side. This was different from the Adam I saw at the hockey rink or lacrosse fields. I had asked my dad to be in the meeting with me as Adam went through all the logistics. I have never been good with money stuff like insurance or investments. Bryan always handled that. My dad could help me with this.

"The insurance companies don't like to pay out what you are owed. It sometimes can get as ridiculous as having to prove that Bryan didn't intentionally get hit or he wasn't riding in the middle of the road," Adam told us. "This is what I do, so let me take care of it."

"I didn't even know we were entitled to something," I told him.

How in the world could anyone think that a person would intentionally put themselves in the ICU, with life-threatening injuries?

"Shauna, I think Adam knows what he is talking about and I think you need to let him handle all of this," my dad said.

So forty-two days after the accident happened, paperwork was signed, and Adam officially became our lawyer. Bryan signed his name on the documents, even though he wouldn't remember doing it. It was a relief to have someone else dealing with all of the legal work.

Adam's work began immediately. He asked me for the following: a picture of Bryan, a copy of our car insurance, and the log-in information for Bryan's "MyChart," which had all of his records.

I hadn't taken any pictures of Bryan up to this point. It wasn't something I had even thought of doing. I didn't want that memory of Bryan lying there helpless, being kept alive with machines, for myself or the kids. Plus, there were signs that said no electronic devices in the ICU and being the rule follower that I am, I didn't bring my phone with me into Bryan's room.

"I haven't taken any pictures of Bryan since the accident, but I'll take a picture of him as soon as I go back to his room," I told Adam. "This will be an easy job to complete. And I'll get you the other things as soon as I can."

"That sounds good. I think that's all for now. If you need anything or have any questions, please don't hesitate to call," he replied as he handed me his card, shut his briefcase, and rose to leave.

"Thank you," my dad said, shaking Adam's hand.

"Thank you for coming, Adam. I feel so relieved that you will handle this for us. It's one less thing I have to worry about," I said.

After my dad and Adam left, I went back to take the picture that Adam requested. When I got to Bryan's room, he was hooked up to the dialysis machine. I snapped a picture, hoping that soon he wouldn't need dialysis.

Later, as I watched them wheel Bryan out the door of the ICU floor on his way to the main trauma floor, my feelings were mixed. I was elated that the doctors felt Bryan was stable enough to move on to the next step on his recovery journey, but I was terrified to leave the security blanket of the ICU. After six weeks, they knew Bryan and had his back. He quickly had become one of their favorite patients. Everyone knew his story and was determined to make him well so he could "ride his bike again." They were there for the good times and the darkest times, so it was difficult to say goodbye to my ICU family. There were hugs and tears.

As we walked away from the ICU, I held my head up and was determined to embrace this new phase of our journey. A thought popped into my mind: *Maybe now that Bryan is moved to the main floor, I won't need to stay twenty-four seven. Maybe I can go home more, spend time with the kids, and sleep in my own bed.* Since the accident, I had an innate feeling that I couldn't go home or leave Bryan for too long. I told myself I would know when it was time. Maybe that time had come.

The transition to the main trauma floor went smoothly. Everyone was extremely accommodating. They brought in two chairs for Shani and me. Each chair could recline into a bed, allowing us to stay in his room. There was also a bathroom in the room. This was a colossal step up from the family lounge. We had our own private space with a real door. I wouldn't have to go through the experience of a nurse coming to remove my belongings again. They made us feel at home.

They explained to me that the nurses weren't right outside the room monitoring everything. The machines that constantly took Bryan's vitals were gone, so the nurses would be coming to take his vitals every three hours. Their station was down the hall, and to get assistance, you had to push the call button. Each nurse was assigned three to four patients, so they couldn't come running at a moment's notice. With Bryan still not able to move his body on his own or talk a lot, I was not comfortable leaving him alone for too long. If he needed help, he might not be able to get it. My thoughts of letting my guard down were quickly squashed. I needed to continue to be his advocate.

After we got settled, I asked the nurse if there was a way to get the code for access to Bryan's "MyChart." Within an hour, I was all set up, another task that Adam needed done. The first time I logged in, I discovered that I could see all the results from his daily blood work, CT scan and X-ray results, and even when his therapies were scheduled. Why wasn't this given to me right away? It would have been extremely helpful. I always had to ask what Bryan's numbers were at his daily meetings. Now I wouldn't have to.

Bryan still was up a lot during the night, so I was "on duty." In the ICU, I had to sleep in the lounge, and the nurses handled everything. Now being in the room with him and not having a one-on-one nurse, I got to do the little things he needed during the night, like adjust his body, move a pillow to a different spot, rub his legs, or get him a sip of water. I hoped that, with fewer interruptions and without the constant hum of the machines, Bryan would be able to get into more of a normal sleep schedule.

Our first morning on the main floor, Bryan tried to eat some breakfast. This meant I had put the Passy-Muir valve on his trach. One bite into his eggs, he started coughing. It sounded as if he were choking, so I took the valve off right away. Then he began to throw up.

Puke is one thing I can't deal with. Blood—yes, guts—yes, puke—NO.

I pressed the nurse call light and held the bucket for him for as long as I could until I started gagging.

"I'm sorry, Bryan, I can't do this," I said as I handed the kidney-shaped basin to him and ran to the bathroom. From the bathroom, I would quickly peek to make sure he was OK but then start gagging again.

Luckily, the nurse didn't take too long to get there. The nurse paged Dr. Beal. When Dr. Beal came in, I explained what happened.

"Maybe we should just take the trach out," he said.

The trach had been one of the main obstacles for Bryan. He needed the valve on to eat and talk, but Bryan continued to say it wasn't getting any easier. If the trach could come out, that would be huge.

"Yes, let's just take it out. Since his oxygen levels are good and he has a strong cough, there really isn't a reason for him to have it anymore," Dr. Beal continued.

Dr. Beal put on some gloves, laid a sterile sheet across Bryan's body from his chin down to his chest, grabbed the end of the trach, and pulled it out right there in the room. It took two seconds for it to come out. I couldn't believe it. How could something that caused so much anxiety and trouble be fixed in two seconds?

Now Bryan would be able to talk normally and breathe easier. Hopefully it would also help with his eating, since there would no longer be a tube down his throat. It was another thing to check off the list of getting Bryan back to "normal," whatever that would be.

Dr. Beal covered the hole in Bryan's throat with some gauze. "The hole will just close on its own in one to two weeks," he told us.

"Really? It's just going to close on its own? The body is an amazing thing," I said.

With the trach, eating and speaking had to be deliberately planned, but now with the trach out, Bryan would be able to eat and speak whenever he wanted. Sadly, Bryan's food intake didn't improve too much. He just didn't feel hungry.

But it was nice to hear Bryan talking more, even if his voice was quieter and a bit raspy. Being able to freely have a conversation with no obstacles was cherished.

Bryan continued to have lots of anxiety, especially around bedtime, and it seemed to be escalating. He fidgeted as much as his body allowed, talked fast, and had rapid breathing. He couldn't explain the reason why this was happening, so Shani and I did what we could. We continued to diffuse essential oils, played relaxing music, and I would massage his arms and legs with lotion or oils since his skin was so dry. The nurses gave him a small nightly dose of Ambien, a sleeping pill, to try and help Bryan sleep for an extended period of time.

Even though there were fewer interruptions than before, the nurses were still scheduled to come in every two hours during the night to move Bryan to prevent bedsores and every three hours to take his vitals. They didn't come in quietly, either. They turned the lights on. Though their voices were at a normal range, in the early hours of the morning, they sounded like they were speaking with megaphones. I consider myself a very quiet, non-confrontational person, but I'd had enough. They kept telling me that he needed to be moved every two hours, but there were times during the day that Bryan wouldn't be moved for up to eight hours, especially when he had dialysis, which was almost a four-hour process from set-up to take-down. So why in the middle of the night did they have it down to the exact minute to come and rotate him?

"Can you please not come in and move Bryan every two hours? He just gets to sleep and you come and move him, then shortly after someone comes in to take his vitals. He's hardly getting any sleep."

"We have to move him every two hours."

"I understand, but can't you come every three hours?"

"NO," the nurse snapped.

I was beyond outraged. The next morning, I went to find the nurse manager, Laurie, a petite woman in her fifties, with short brown hair and glasses. I found her standing at the nurses' station.

She smiled. "Is there something I can help you with?" she asked in her quiet, gentle voice.

"Would it be possible to cluster Bryan's care during the night to every three hours so everything can be done at the same time? Bryan is hardly sleeping. Right now it seems like they are coming in all the time. I think this would really help. I know he has to be moved. I will sign something that says we take responsibility if he gets any bed sores. But Bryan needs to sleep," I said. "Also, every time the nurses come in, they turn on the lights and talk loudly."

"Of course, we can do that," she said. "I'll talk with the night nurses and remind them that, even though it's their daytime, it's the middle of the night for the patients. I'll put it in Bryan's chart that his cares will be clustered every three hours or if he calls before then."

I was so grateful and relieved that she was so kind, though I wondered why the nurses would have to be reminded to lower their voices in the middle of the night. "Thank you so much. We really appreciate it."

That night, the same nurse from the night before was our nurse, and she was a bit standoffish. "We will be coming in every three hours."

"Thank you," I said smiling.

"It won't be my fault if he gets any sores," she said under her breath.

Part of me wanted to tell her where to stick it. She had no idea what happened all day long. Sometimes the protocols have to be altered to best meet the needs of the individual patient. I bit my tongue and didn't say a thing.

From that night on, Bryan's sleep improved a little. He usually woke up before the three hours was up to get moved anyway, but at least it was on his timeline rather than a forced two-hour regimen.

Bryan again began bringing up the accident. He was trying to understand what happened. Thank goodness he didn't remember anything from the actual accident. How would he ever bike again if he did? He kept saying, "I can't believe I got hit. I thought I was more observant."

"It's hard to be observant when someone hits you from behind," I said. I felt a flush of anger at the person who hit him and left him to die. "You can't look back every time a vehicle is going to pass you.

The nephrologist came in every few days to give an update on Bryan's kidneys. He looked at Bryan's creatinine and BUN (blood urea nitrogen) levels, which had been showing improvement. From the beginning, I'd been holding onto what I'd been told over and over, "His kidneys will just turn back on when they are ready."

But today, Bryan's forty-fifth day in the hospital, the nephrologist said, "Bryan's numbers have been stagnant for six weeks. If things don't change, we'll have to find another course of action. Let's wait a few more days."

My positive bubble burst. *What does that mean? A kidney transplant? What else do they do for non-functioning kidneys besides dialysis?* Just what I needed, a new worry.

Bryan's kidneys must have heard the nephrologist talking badly about them, because not even twenty-four hours later, they gave the nephrologist a big FU. Bryan peed! That was what we had been praying for since day one. The kidneys started to wake up. He would still need to continue to have dialysis until his kidney numbers were lower—kidneys have to produce a lot of urine to get them working properly—but it was a glimmer of hope.

Peeing turned into quite an ordeal. It not only hurt every time Bryan peed, but we had to navigate the use of the hard plastic urinal. The urinal reminded me of a plastic milk jug with a slight bend on the top. Unfortunately, it didn't bend like a milk jug. Bryan's testicles had become so swollen that it made navigating the act of peeing extremely difficult. To try and manipulate the penis out from the testicles and position it into the urinal correctly was almost impossible. There were many times his penis would slip out of my grasp before he finished peeing. I would wrap the blanket around him so he could continue to pee. However, that meant a sponge bath and change of sheets and gown, which was a whole ordeal on its own.

It got to the point that Bryan knew he needed to pee but physically couldn't go, so the nurse would use a one-time catheterization tube on him. Each time, she would get anywhere from eight hundred to one thousand milliliters of urine, around four cups. This was now happening every time Bryan had to go to the bathroom, so they decided to put a catheter that could stay in and be connected to a bag. Bryan was relieved he didn't have to continue to make his immobile body move into a pee position. It would just come out on its own.

One night around midnight, Bryan woke me up. "Shauna, I pooped."

I thought I was dreaming. "What?"

"I think I pooped."

"Bryan, you couldn't have. Your intestines are not connected to your butthole."

"But I did."

"OK, let me check." I turned on some lights, and sure enough there was a diarrhea-like discharge all over the sheets. I pushed the call button for a clean-up. "You were right."

"I told you."

How was that even possible? The doctor had closed his rectal stump, and the other end was on his right side emptying into a bag. I hoped it didn't mean something was leaking. The next morning at Bryan's daily meeting, I informed the doctors.

"Yes, that can happen," said Dr. Farhat. "The rectum is a living tissue, so it will continue to produce mucus even though it is not 'hooked up' to anything. There's nothing to be worried about. This may happen from time to time."

"I'm glad there isn't anything to be worried about, but it would have been nice to know that might occur. It was very concerning last night when we didn't know what was happening."

"I'm sure it was alarming. Sorry we never mentioned it, but there really is nothing to worry about."

Later that day, Bob, a coworker of Bryan's, delivered Bryan his new phone. His old phone was broken in the accident. This opened a new line of communication for Bryan. I could rest a bit easier when I left the room, knowing he could reach me. I always made sure his phone was in reach before I would leave so he could text me if he needed anything.

Bryan's dad was happy to learn about Bryan getting a new phone. Now he could communicate solely with Bryan and not have to go through me, which was good because we had a disagreement during a recent visit. After Jan had returned to the car, Steve started talking about her driving again.

I'd had enough. Every time he came to visit, we discussed this. I knew that taking the keys away from Jan was admitting that her dementia had progressed significantly, something Steve was unable to process. But the stress of Bryan's situation put a limit on how much patience I had for another talk. It was going to have to be up to him to take action. It seemed obvious to me considering all of the decisions I had to make on behalf of Bryan in the last fifty-seven days. "I am done with this conversation!" I said sternly, pointing my finger at him. "If Jan hurts someone, like someone did to Bryan, it will be your fault." He didn't bring it up again.

The phone didn't provide the relief I had hoped. I soon discovered that I couldn't stay away too long before I would get a text from Bryan. Keep in mind that I never left him alone for more than thirty minutes, usually only to go down to the cafeteria to eat, visit the gift shop, or walk outside to the corner and back for some fresh air.

Regardless, there would be a text. "When are you coming back?" Bryan's sense of time had changed when he fell asleep. He would think hours had passed, but it typically was only a few minutes in real time.

I guess it was nice to know he wanted/needed me there, but sometimes I just needed to get out of his room to regroup and see a different view other than the four walls of Bryan's room, looking out the window at the lit-up words "North Memorial."

"I'll be right back," I answered and rushed back to his room.

That is why I stayed.

Chapter 21

Bryan's white blood count continued to go up and down, which indicated that there was an infection somewhere. But no matter how many tests the doctors ran, they couldn't find the source. *Is it in his lungs? Urine? Heart? Or is it located in one of the many tubes sticking in his body?* I couldn't understand how no source could be found. It was not only frustrating, but very worrisome.

At one point, the infectious disease doctor put Bryan in an isolation protocol. That meant that any hospital worker coming into his room had to put a gown, mask, and gloves on. This created a barrier between the doctor and the germs. I was never told why he was put in isolation. I imagine since they couldn't find the source of infection, they didn't want to risk any cross-contamination of germs spreading to other patients. Luckily, there were no changes in protocols for me or any of our visitors besides washing our hands before entering the room, which we had been doing since day one.

Infections are what kill patients, kept echoing in my head.

One nurse told me, "Maybe Bryan's white blood count is elevated from all the trauma and stress his body has gone through and not from an infection."

Is that possible? I prayed that was the reason but was thankful the doctors were continuing to test, test, test.

Bryan was scheduled for transesophageal echocardiography (TEE). This test gives more details about the heart than a regular echocardiogram. The doctors needed to make sure an infection hadn't gone to his heart. As a part of the test, Bryan needed to swallow a small camera, which would allow them to get a clearer picture of the heart through his throat. The camera was in a pill that was attached to a cord. When they were done, they would pull the camera out.

I was very concerned about Bryan being able to swallow a pill since he really hadn't swallowed anything more than a nibble of food since his second swallow test, which had upgraded him to a soft food diet with blended meats. I didn't know how they were going to get him to swallow a large pill.

As we waited for transport to take Bryan to his test, he told me about a vision he'd had about being on a boat.

"You and I were on a boat for four days. They told me that I needed to die to save the jellyfish."

"What?" I said. "Maybe that's where your mind took you when you were on life support. Maybe the sounds of the machines made you think you were on a boat?"

They came to get him for the test, so I'd have to wait for further explanation on the vision he'd had. After they wheeled him out of the room, I couldn't shake the image. It was amazing what our bodies could endure and how our minds worked through the trauma.

When he was done with the test and back in his room, all he could say was, "That was close to awful."

"You did it though. Nice work."

The tests came back the following day, and his heart looked perfect—what a relief. The last thing we needed was something affecting his heart.

Enough of his organs were damaged already. We were still working on getting the kidneys, the liver, the stomach, and what was left of his intestines back to normal.

Bryan's abdominal hernia, which had been covered with a piece of mesh, needed to be covered with a skin graft. I had heard of skin grafts but didn't know the logistics.

"A skin graft is quite the process," Shelly explained to me, her nursing skills once again coming in handy. "They will take a machine, like a wood planter, to scrape off a thin top layer of skin from the top of Bryan's thigh. Then they put that skin through a machine that will poke holes in it, kind of like a pasta press."

The image of his skin going through a pasta press made me gag, but I nodded.

"This will make the skin look like mesh. Then they will sew that harvested skin over his abdominal opening. The holes allow the fluid to drain from under the graft in hopes that the graft will not be rejected. As the skin heals, the holes will fill in."

In his pre-op description, Dr. Evans said, "I'll take off the mesh that we placed over Bryan's abdomen twenty-four days ago and then sew the skin graft over the same area the mesh was covering. In six to twelve months, Bryan could possibly have another surgery to reverse the ileostomy."

I hadn't heard about an ileostomy reversal before. I didn't want to dwell on it, but that was an exciting revelation. It gave me hope that Bryan might not have to poop in a bag for the rest of his life. I would put that thought on the back burner and ask about it later.

Bryan went into surgery around 10:20 a.m. While he was in surgery, I got caught up on my journaling. So much happened in one day that, if I didn't write it down, I would forget. I went down to the cafeteria to grab a bite to eat and seized the opportunity of some alone time to take a nap. On nights that Bryan didn't sleep, which was frequent, I didn't sleep, either.

Around 2:00 p.m., Dr. Evans came to tell me that the surgery had gone well. "Bryan will be a little sore."

"It can't be worse than getting hit by a truck," I said, laughing.

I even got a chuckle out of Dr. Evans who was usually very stoic and matter-of-fact.

When Bryan came back from surgery, his left thigh was covered in bloody bandages. You could see where the strips of skin had been scraped off. His abdomen was covered with a wound vac, which helped accelerate the growing of new tissue and heal the area. I was still amazed by how much his body had been through.

Chapter 22

In January, I had signed up to coach Elyse's track team on Saturday afternoons beginning in the spring but didn't know if I was going to be able to keep this commitment now. I didn't want to let Elyse down, and coaching her team would give me that time to reconnect with her each week. Gregg was coming to see Bryan every weekend, so maybe we could work something out. I called to ask him.

"Absolutely, Shauna. I'm glad you feel comfortable leaving him in my hands," he said.

With Gregg's guarantee, I could move forward with my plans to coach. We agreed that, when he arrived on Saturday mornings, I would give him a quick update and then head home. I would have my "freedom" from nine to five.

That started my new Saturday routine. When I got home, I would go for a run. Working out is something that is a huge part of my life. Training for the upcoming triathlon season had come to an abrupt halt. Being able to go for a run again, even once a week, was a needed recharge. But I wasn't prepared for how much endurance I had lost. It felt like I had never run before. But since my training had been derailed, it didn't really matter how fast I could run. Instead, I relished the fresh air, the chance to move my body and escape from my reality for those precious thirty-five minutes each week.

And I savored every minute of the short time the kids and I had together. I wanted to hear about what they had been doing that week. They talked about their friends, showed me some of their schoolwork, etc. I would quickly go through the mail, read the stack of cards, and pay bills before we had lunch.

After lunch, Elyse and I would head to track. Griffin stayed home with my parents because, with all of the events and heats for each event, track lasted for three hours. Since we lived close by, I could text my parents when Elyse's events were going to start and they could get there quickly. Griffin didn't complain too much about being dragged along, since he always found friends to run around with when he was there.

After track, I packed myself fresh clothes and gathered any items I needed for the week ahead. Another week of living at the hospital. It had been fifty-four days. I wondered when I would get to stay home and not be packing my bags. Not this week.

When it was time to leave, I gave the kids and my parents hugs and kisses with a couple of extra squeezes for the kids.

"Be good. I'll see you next week," I told them.

They all stood in the driveway to wave goodbye. It broke my heart to drive away each week.

On my way back to the hospital, I would pick up something for Gregg and me for dinner from a restaurant or the Cub Foods near the hospital.

One Saturday after track, I ran into Janelle in the hospital parking lot. Her son was doing really well and was going to be transferred to Gillette Children's Hospital for therapy. We chatted about how Bryan was doing. I told her we were still taking it day by day.

Near the end of our conversation, she smiled and said, "I don't know who to give my key necklace to."

Odd that it had only been two weeks since I had passed the "HOPE" necklace on to her. It felt like a lifetime ago. "That's exactly what I thought until you came along," I said smiling back. "Just keep it. You will know when you are supposed to pass it on."

We hugged and wished each other well. Each of us had gone through terrible life-changing traumas but came out on the other side. We connected on Facebook, so we would be able to continue to follow each other's journeys.

Later that evening, I got an unexpected call from my mom. My mind always jumped to the worst.

"Shauna, there was a terrible accident somewhere near your house," she said, and I could hear the tension in her voice. We later found out that, at an intersection near our house, there was a deadly car accident. "There were so many emergency vehicles coming from all directions with their sirens never ending. It sounded like they were in your backyard. Griffin was beyond terrified. He kept saying, 'What's that? What's wrong? What's going on?' He was panicking. I comforted him the best I could. I think you need to talk to him."

"Of course, I'll talk to him," I said, my heart breaking for my little guy. How would this trauma we'd all been through look for each of us down the line? I was still nowhere near being able to process it all.

"On a lighter note," my mom continued, "Elyse told him: 'Griffin, Dad is already in the hospital. Mom is with him and we are all here, so what are you worried about?'" A typical Elyse statement.

"Oh goodness. She tells it like it is, doesn't she? Can you put Griff on the phone?"

"Sure. Love you."

"Love you too, Mom. Thanks."

"Hi, Griff."

"Hi, Mom." His voice sounded so small.

"Meme told me about all the sirens you heard."

"Yeah, it was really scary," he said. "Someone must have gotten hurt like Dad."

"I can imagine how scary it was to hear. We are all OK. Meme and Papa will take care of you."

"I know, but the sirens scared me."

"It's OK to be scared. Every time I hear them, I get scared, too. Try to get some sleep, and I will talk to you in the morning."

"OK."

"I love you, Griffin."

"Love you too, Mom."

The next morning, my mom would tell me that, after I talked with Griffin, he was more reassured, but he needed some extra cuddles before he would finally lie down to sleep.

I knew we wouldn't understand the ramifications of Bryan's accident on Griffin and Elyse in the future. It was a part of their lives and would affect them forever. One can never know what a trigger will be until it happens. Then we would have to be ready to deal with it, myself included.

Chapter 23

From early on in our journey, we had been getting information for two rehabilitation centers in the Twin Cities area that Bryan could go to: Bethesda and Regency. The rehabilitation center was the next step in Bryan's care. We needed a center that would be able to handle Bryan's medical needs, dialysis, and his abdominal issues, along with all the OT and PT therapies he would need.

After much discussion and weighing the pros and cons, Bryan and I had chosen Bethesda. It was located in Saint Paul, which was closer to home, only about fifteen minutes away. This would allow the kids to see us more. It was even possible I would be able to stay at home and go visit Bryan during the day. It would be a small step back to normalcy. I could get the kids ready for school in the morning, but instead of going to work, I would go to be with Bryan. Then I would be back at night to tuck them in. Just imagining all of this felt refreshing.

Before Bryan could be transferred to a rehab center, Dr. Farhat told me that they needed to put in a PICC line for TPN. They had been using his central line in his neck. The PICC line would be placed in his arm and would allow Bryan to move more easily when he started the intense therapy sessions twice a day. Getting the PICC line gave me a glimmer of hope that Bryan was closer to being home.

Before they could put in the PICC line, a CT scan needed to be done to make sure everything was clear and infection free. Bryan's white blood count continued to be high, but still nothing had been found.

Unfortunately, the CT scan results this time showed fluid around Bryan's lungs. The PICC line would have to be put on hold. One step forward, two steps back—I tried not to feel discouraged.

I tried to look on the bright side. Draining the fluid from around the lungs would help Bryan breathe easier. He had been coughing up so much mucus and phlegm. Many times he would cough so hard, he would gag and then throw up. The doctors had increased his respiratory therapy sessions, which included nebulizers to help loosen the mucus and lung exercises to increase the strength of his cough.

But when Bryan would be really congested, the respiratory therapist would put a tube up his nose, down his throat, and into his lungs. Then they would turn on the suction and vacuum some of the mucus out to help clear his lungs. The process was terrible to witness. When they would turn the suction on, his body would become rigid as he arched his back, with all of his air being sucked out. It looked like an exorcism. I only witnessed this procedure once—that was one too many times.

A bronchoscopy was ordered so they could see inside his lungs and get samples of the mucus and tissue to test for infection. An ultrasound and an EKG on Bryan's heart were also done to see if there was any fluid around it. I was feeling confident his heart was fine. They had just done the echocardiogram nine days earlier, and everything was clear.

After all the tests were done and we were waiting for the results, the occupational and physical therapists came in. They wanted to get Bryan into a wheelchair and have him attempt to wheel himself down the hall. I stood behind Bryan and the therapists, watching. His emaciated yellowish gray arms slowly pushed him forward. Bryan looked back at me with his bulging eyes, tears streaming down his cheeks as he slowly propelled himself down the end of the hall. He was so proud to be doing something by himself. He only got halfway down the hall when, unfortunately, we got called back to his room. The cardiologist needed to talk with us.

Can't we just have one moment of happiness? If the cardiologist needs to talk to us, it can't be good.

When we returned to Bryan's room, Dr. King, the cardiologist, was waiting for us. "Bryan, you have fluid around your heart that we have to remove. The fluid can cause lots of trouble for the heart and can even be fatal if not taken care of."

"What? You have got to be kidding me," I said, knowing that he wasn't. "This is not what we were expecting. Everything was fine nine days ago." *Shit! The one organ that we hadn't been worried about, now we have to worry about.*

"The procedure we will do is called a pericardial window," Dr. King explained. "I will cut a small opening into the sac that surrounds the heart to drain the fluid. I will insert a tube to let the fluid continue to drain for a few days." Dr. King looked from Bryan to me and back to Bryan. "I know this is not what you wanted to hear. I want to assure you that this is a very simple procedure and something that needs to be done. I will take good care of Bryan."

Bryan nodded.

I was more frustrated than concerned. *We are getting him ready to go to rehab. How long would this set him back?*

Instead of moving to rehab, Bryan was scheduled for two separate surgeries: to drain the lung and to drain the fluid around his heart.

The chest tube would be put in first. When fluid surrounds your lungs, your lungs can't move and get enough oxygen. I was encouraging Bryan, telling him that this would help him breathe more easily.

There should have been a drastic improvement, but I couldn't have been more wrong. When Bryan got back from surgery and they were moving him back to his bed, he started screaming and crying in agony. Moving him into bed caused agitation to the chest tube, which was extremely painful. In all the time Bryan was in the hospital, with all that he had been through, I had never heard him utter a word of complaint about anything, including pain. It was horrible to witness him in so much distress.

"Help him!" I cried.

The nurse had to order Dilaudid, a painkiller, which seemed to take an eternity. She had to enter all the details of the order into the computer, wait for it to be sent up from the pharmacy, go to the nurses' station to get it, and finally administer the medication to Bryan.

"The tube must have moved when we transferred him to his bed. It can be painful," the nurse explained to me.

"I guess so!"

In the meantime, Bryan's pleas for help were heartbreaking. There was nothing I could do to take away his pain. I just stood there helpless, crying, watching him writhe in agony. It was fifteen minutes after she gave Bryan the shot before it kicked in and Bryan calmed down. He fell asleep, exhausted from the episode.

From that point on and throughout the next week, Bryan would be terrified he would experience that pain again. He would barely move, cough, breathe deeply, or even talk. He lay as still and silent as possible, like he was frozen, even when he was awake. It made doing his PT and OT a bit difficult.

They kept him pretty doped up on pain meds for the night so he could sleep and be ready for heart surgery in the morning.

The next morning, Bryan awoke really agitated. He was supposed to have the drain put in his heart, but nothing I said to him would calm him down. Why would it? Yesterday I had told him how great the chest tube would be and how he would be breathing so much better. We know how that turned out. He didn't want to go through that experience again, and neither did I.

"I don't want to have this surgery," he said. "I don't want to hurt like that again."

"I know, Bryan, but you have to have the fluid drained from around your heart."

He turned his head and wouldn't even look at me. Talk about a mix of emotions—on one hand, I wanted to cry because there was nothing I could say or do to help him. On the other hand, I wanted to scream at him, "Don't take it out on me! This is what has to be done!" I chose to sit quietly and let him deal with it on his own.

Luckily, they came bright and early, so there wasn't too much time to perseverate on the heart surgery and the potential pain another drain tube might cause.

In hindsight, I look back on that day and realize that I should have been more worried. But I was so numb from all the procedures and surgeries over the past sixty days that it just didn't register. Bryan was having HEART surgery. I acted like it was a routine tonsillectomy, no big deal.

Bryan was scheduled to stay in the cardiac ICU for one night. The sixth floor was going to hold his room for us, so we didn't have to pack all of our things up.

My parents dropped the kids off at school and hurried to the hospital so I wouldn't have to sit alone during the surgery. We were in the same waiting area I was in that first horrible night. It was a bit eerie, so I tried to not let my mind go back there. It helped having my parents there. We discussed the kids' upcoming activities and updated the family calendar.

"Shauna, let's go get a snack and something to drink," my dad suggested. "Mom will stay here in case the doctor comes. She can text us."

"OK, sounds good."

We didn't say too much on our walk. It was a nice distraction from what was happening. My dad is a quiet, gentleman whose presence puts people at ease. We quickly picked out a snack and headed back because I didn't want to be gone too long.

Dr. King was coming out of the door just as we approached the waiting room.

"The heart surgery went smoothly. We removed eight hundred cc's from around his heart and left a drain in," Dr. King informed us.

Eight hundred cc's is three-and-a-half cups! I felt a wave of relief. "Thank you for everything," I said.

Dr. King told us we could head up to the cardiac ICU waiting room on the fifth floor to wait for Bryan to be out of recovery and back in his room. So we headed up to the waiting room, and after making sure I was OK, my parents left to pick the kids up at school.

As I waited to be called back to see Bryan, I updated his CaringBridge page:

> This morning, Bryan had surgery to drain the fluid from around his heart. Now he has two additional drains with gallon-sized bags attached to him. He will stay in the cardiac ICU for one night to be monitored.

Almost immediately after I posted the update, I received a text message from Bryan's sister, Gina. "Tell my little brother I love him," she wrote.

What the hell? I was furious. *Where has she been since she is here to visit?* After all this time and all the procedures and surgeries, I had gotten nothing, not a call, not an email, not a text. If she really cared, she would have contacted me before this. I couldn't even answer her back. I would have said something I would have regretted.

The time in the cardiac ICU was uneventful, which was a pleasant blessing. Bryan was wiped out from the back-to-back surgeries. It was unsettling to see him hooked up to all the monitoring machines again, but it eased my mind knowing that the nurses and doctors were right outside the room. When you are in the ICU, you are constantly being observed.

Bryan was resting peacefully, so when Kathy and Bill brought their weekly dinner to me, we decided to go outside to eat. It was a hot ninety-two degrees. It was nice to feel the warmth, sunshine, and fresh air after a long taxing day. They only stayed as long as it took to eat dinner. They knew I needed to get back to Bryan's room. It was a relief to get out of the hospital atmosphere, even for only a half hour.

At 9:00 that evening, the nurse came into the room and asked, "What time are you leaving?"

"Umm, I stay with him."

"I'll have to check with the charge nurse. We don't usually let people stay."

"Oh, OK," I said nervously. *Oh shit, what if they don't let me stay? Can I go sleep in his room on the sixth floor? That would be too far away from Bryan.* "I can just sleep in a chair in the waiting room," I added.

When the nurse finally came back, I held my breath waiting for her answer.

"You can stay."

"Thank you so much. I really appreciate it. He hasn't been alone for the sixty days since his accident. Thank you."

I tried to blend in as much as possible and not let them know I was even there. I hardly heard the nurses during the night. They came in so quietly and moved Bryan so gently. I had woken up about 2:00 a.m. and had to go to the bathroom but didn't want to leave Bryan's room and get in trouble, so I held it for hours until closer to the morning.

The day after Bryan's heart surgery marked two months since the accident. It was also Mother's Day. Erica and I decided that, since it was going to be a beautiful sunny day, we could celebrate in the little park behind the hospital. My parents brought the kids after Griffin's lacrosse game. On their way over from Chippewa Falls, Erica and my nieces stopped at a nearby Popeyes to pick up some chicken and fries. We sat at the picnic table and ate.

When we were done, the kids gave me presents to open. Elyse picked out two Snoopy bracelets. One had pink Snoopys and the other had gray. My mom said, "When Elyse saw these at Michael's, she insisted on getting them for you." Griffin's gift was a plaque that said, "You are the best!"

My heart was overflowing with happiness. I was so proud to be their mom.

Bryan was really tired and groggy, so we took turns going up to say hi and see him. You could tell he was not in the mood for visitors. He hardly even looked at anyone and kept his eyes closed most of the time, so the visits were short. The kids spent the rest of the afternoon playing on the playground equipment. Before we knew, it was time to say goodbye. It was a nice Mother's Day for my mom, my sister, and me. I hated for it to end, because for those few brief hours, life almost seemed normal. I turned and walked back through the doors of the hospital and up to Bryan's room.

Chapter 24

After two months in the hospital, we needed to make a final decision where Bryan would do his rehab. "PT Paul," as we fondly called him, pushed for us to stay and finish his rehab at North Memorial. We really didn't know this was even a choice. We had only been given the options of Bethesda and Regency. Paul explained that all of Bryan's therapists would remain the same. The focus would center around his therapy. Before this point, all Bryan's medical issues were the top priority and therapy always came after that. Once on the rehab floor, OT and PT sessions would be scheduled twice a day and everything would be scheduled around that.

Paul requested someone from the rehab floor to come and talk with us. They had to determine if Bryan would qualify to stay at North Memorial for rehab. After answering some questions and looking through his charts, they believed that he would definitely qualify to stay. They questioned if he would even qualify to go to Bethesda anymore because he was medically stable.

Bryan and I weighed all of our options and made the decision to stay at North Memorial. We were disappointed we wouldn't be closer to the kids, but staying at North Memorial was the best for Bryan. The entire staff knew him. If he were to have a medical setback, the trauma doctors could swoop in. That eased both of our minds. There were only three weeks left of school until summer break, so this would make it more flexible for the kids to visit.

Now that Bryan would be going to the seventh floor, he would have been on every floor of the hospital except for the third, which was the maternity floor. We joked that Bryan was a miracle, but if he had been admitted to that floor, he would have indeed been the "ultimate miracle."

During this whole ordeal, Bryan received over fifty blood transfusions. He would have died multiple times without them. We needed to do something to pay back what was done for him. One easy way was to host blood drives. There were three blood drives set up in Bryan's name. Both of our workplaces arranged blood drives, and Shani scheduled one in Chippewa Falls.

The first time I went back to school since the accident was the day of the blood drive. My dad arrived at the hospital at 5:30 a.m. to stay with Bryan. This gave me enough time to stop at home and shower before heading there. I couldn't believe how nervous I was to see everyone. These were my colleagues and friends, but I had been living in a bubble for seventy-one days and now I would be thrust into being the center of attention. It was something I did not like. To add to my jitters, the Saint Paul Pioneer Press was going to be there taking pictures. I had talked with Nick Ferraro, a reporter from the paper a few days earlier. He had come to the hospital to interview me about our story and wanted to write an article about how our community "wrapped its arms" around us.

I intentionally scheduled my blood donation appointment for 8:45 a.m., during the time the students arrived at school. This would allow them to get settled before I went to visit. It was incredible to witness so many people coming to donate blood, and for many, it was their first time. Even the detective working on Bryan's case came to donate. I wish I could have stayed to thank everyone individually, but time didn't allow for that. I was on a tight schedule as I wanted to be back at the hospital by 10:30 a.m.

After donating blood, I walked down the hall to my classroom. When they saw me, my students ran and surrounded me in a big group hug, and because I needed an individual hug from each of them, I had them form a line. Then, one by one, I received some of the biggest hugs I have ever gotten. We also did a jiggle break together, where we danced around the room to get their wiggles out before they would have to sit and begin their lessons.

It was exactly what I needed. I missed these kiddos and being their teacher. I was torn between two worlds. There was nothing more I wanted to do than to be their teacher. It would have been easy to start our daily morning routines and have everything seem normal again. But the reality was that wouldn't happen. I couldn't stay because I needed to leave and go back to the hospital. It was my sole purpose right now. As I left the room saying my last goodbye, I could hear shouts of "Bye, Mrs. Joas," "I love you, Mrs. Joas," and "I'll miss you" as I walked down the hall and out the door.

Walking to my car, I reflected on how this school year had been turned upside down. So even though the time was brief, it was a relief to be there with them. They could see with their own eyes that I was OK. We could smile and laugh as we hugged and danced together.

I knew, as I drove back, it would be a busy day. They were getting Bryan ready to move to the rehab floor. Another transition, which was always worrisome—all new procedures to learn, people to meet, change in schedules. But this would be the last step until we went home. The light was getting brighter. We were on the homestretch of this journey. Bryan had overcome and conquered so many obstacles. Now it was time to get strong and learn how to live outside the hospital.

When I got back, I was thrilled to see that Bryan's chest tube had been taken out. It had been in for thirteen days. That was much longer than they intended, but they had to wait until the volume of what was draining out decreased. Every tube removed was a step forward in Bryan's recovery.

The doctors had been holding off on doing dialysis for over a week. They needed to watch the kidney and blood level numbers to see if they remained stable. They had, so now his dialysis port was removed. NO MORE DIALYSIS. His kidneys did just what the doctors said they would during the first days of Bryan's journey. "The kidneys are really sensitive. They will turn back on when they are ready." I couldn't believe it. Again, I was floored by the power of the human body.

Bryan's catheter came out, too, so he would have to pee in the urinal again. The last step to get him ready for rehab was putting his PICC line in. Now he was ready for moving day. There was so much positivity in one day. I had to pinch myself to make sure it was all true.

Bryan's paperwork was approved for his transfer to the rehab floor. Even though we were in the same hospital, the seventh floor felt like a different world. The policy, on the rehab floor, was for all the patients to wear clothes—goodbye hospital gowns. I would need to go shopping and get Bryan some larger shirts and pants, since his stomach was still so swollen.

Down the hall from Bryan's room, there was a family lounge with a refrigerator, stove, and microwave. Across the hall from the lounge, there was a washer and dryer. They wanted it to feel like home. There was a chair that converted into a bed for me in his room. The best part of the move I thought was that Bryan would get to take a shower—a real shower—three times a week. I knew how good it felt to take a nice warm shower to energize you, and it would be something normal.

"You aren't sick anymore," Nurse Karen told Bryan.

This was hard to believe because for so long we were told, "You are really sick." He had required so much medical care that this new mindset was scary but invigorating. This comment flipped the switch for Bryan. It gave him that mental boost of confidence he needed to endure the rigor of the intense therapy.

Therapy would be two times a day with a lunch break in between. The morning would start early with OT. Becca would come in to help Bryan get dressed, brush his teeth, and shave, teaching him how to do his own self-care.

Previously, they had been using a Hoyer lift, a sling-like apparatus that transfers a patient from point A to point B, for transferring Bryan from bed to wheelchair, since he had no strength. It was hard to witness Bryan dangling helplessly as they moved him.

Now Becca would introduce the slide board. It would be a new way to transfer himself. Slide boards are approximately two feet long. A non-weight-bearing patient like Bryan uses it to transfer from one place to another. He had to put the board under his bottom and then use his upper body to scoot himself across to the destination. At first he was belted for safety so Becca could guide him. Then when his balance and upper body strength improved, he would lose the belt and do it on his own.

It didn't take long for Bryan to get the hang of his self-care, so by the middle of the first week, Becca no longer had to come to help him in the morning. He would brush his teeth, shave, and get dressed, with just a little help from me. He would transfer himself to the wheelchair and wheel himself to the elevator and down to the therapy room. There Becca would meet him to work on his fine motor skills, coordination, and mental endurance. He had to push lights on a big lightboard, using both his right and left hand for hand-and-eye coordination. He used resistance bands and a hand bike to strengthen his arms and hands. They would play games on the iPad that challenged his mental cognition. The OT session lasted about an hour.

Then Paul, the PT, would take Bryan to the physical therapy area and go through some stretching, strength exercises, wheelchair mobility, and slide board transfers. There were real beds to practice going from wheelchair to bed and vice versa. There was even a real car to practice going from wheelchair to car. The PT session lasted about an hour and a half.

Then one of the many helpers at the hospital would wheel Bryan back up to his room for a lunch break. He would eat a little and then take a short rest. He only had about a ninety-minute break, and then he would have to go back downstairs to do his second round of OT and PT for the day. Although it was exhausting and took everything he had, Bryan knew this was the only way for him to go home. For this reason, he willingly embraced the therapy sessions without complaint.

The day after Bryan got on the rehab floor, he had his first shower, the first one in seventy-three days. I was so excited for him. Sponge baths and the amazing shampoo-filled shower caps were now a thing of the past. I imagined how wonderful it would feel. I knew how good it felt to take a shower after a weekend of no showers; I could only imagine after seventy-three days . . . Still being non-weight bearing, he had to be transferred to a shower chair and then be taken to the shower room.

When the nurse brought him back, I was eager to see how it went. I asked, "So . . . how was it? Wonderful?"

"It was horrible," Bryan said, grimacing. "I was freezing. Can you give me a shower next time?"

"How could it have been horrible?"

"The nurse was so slow. The water only hit one part of my body at a time. I was so cold. Maybe I should just stick to sponge baths."

"I'm sorry. Let's try having me give you a shower next time and see if it is any better. We will figure this out."

I thought the shower was going to be so wonderful. What I imagined versus reality was completely the opposite—another bubble burst.

When it was time for Bryan's next shower, I needed to learn the procedure. It was really hard to see Bryan so vulnerable and dependent on me. He kept saying, "I'm so sorry you have to do this." All the modesty went out the window for him. I am sure this was not what he wanted his wife to be doing for him.

There was so much prep work before the actual shower: taking off Bryan's shirt and then covering his PICC line port, the ileostomy bag, and feeding tube with plastic wrap and two-sided tape to keep it all dry. I was nervous I was doing everything wrong. Tape was everywhere. *Is this really going to keep all the water out of his lines? What would happen if water did get into them?* I hoped we wouldn't have to find out.

Once that was all done, he would transfer himself to the shower chair. Then we would take off his pants. Since he couldn't stand, undressing him while sitting in a chair was quite an event. Bryan had to rock back and forth as I shimmied his pants under his butt until I could pull them off.

It was shocking seeing Bryan sitting there. It was the first time I had seen him completely naked. I knew he was skinny, but it was like looking at a skeleton, only he had gray-toned skin covering him. His bony legs were limp and dangled as if he was a small child sitting in a chair that was too big for his feet to touch the floor. But there wasn't anything I wouldn't do for this man, wherever the road would lead us. We would get through this together. Look how far we had already come.

I tried to wash one part at a time, starting with his head and working my way down. After I would finish washing an area, I would cover him with a towel. If someone would have recorded that first shower, we certainly would have made it on America's funniest videos. Water and soap were everywhere. Bottles were dropped. I was a fumbling idiot. By the time we were done, I looked as if I had taken a shower, too. Eventually we would become more efficient.

In every hospital room, there was a whiteboard that had the patient's name, the date, times of therapy, any meds given, notes to the other staff, and a discharge date. Up until this time, Bryan's discharge date was blank. But now, there it was, as if it were flashed up on a movie marquee shining for all to see: JUNE 3 (day eighty-eight). I never thought this day would come. When this journey started, all I could think about was it being over, getting out of the haunted house, not looking over my shoulder for the next scare, and finally being able to breathe again.

Now, with the discharge date set, I had to step up my game. When Bryan would go down to therapy, I worked on getting things ready for us to go home. There was a lot to do: ramps to get into the house and a ramp to get into our sunken living room, a makeshift bedroom on the main level, and the biggest thing . . . a shower.

We HAD a shower in the main floor bathroom, but I always thought, *Who needs a shower on the main floor?* We had two showers upstairs and one shower in the basement, so all that we really needed was a half bath. So about two weeks before the accident, Bryan decided to start remodeling the main floor bathroom. He tore out the shower, along with the wall that separated the bathroom from the kitchen. It left a gaping hole that exposed you every time you needed to use the toilet, which would have been fine for us until the remodel was completed. But that remodel was put on hold because of the accident. Our neighbor, John, put up some plywood so people could use the bathroom in the meantime. Now that we were coming home, we needed the shower back. We asked Bryan's dad, who has lots of home improvement skills, to install a makeshift temporary shower. One of Bryan's old classmates donated a shower for us to reinstall.

I also had to learn how to change all of Bryan's bandages and ileostomy bag, clean his feeding tube, feed him through the feeding tube, and learn his medication schedule. There was so much to do. *How would I manage all of this at home on my own?* I also felt there was a need to talk to the insurance company to make sure all the nurses and therapies needed were covered when we went home. I also worked on writing thank-you notes to everyone who supported us during this ordeal. My mom had instilled in me the importance of sending a personalized thank-you note to show your appreciation, and I had never been more appreciative.

After therapies, Bryan and I just hung out in his room watching movies. Bryan brought up the idea of getting a dog. Everyone in our family loved dogs, but we hadn't had a dog since Griffin was six months old. That was when Bryan had to put his dog of fourteen years down. Afterwards he said, "I'm never going to go through that again." Griffin and Elyse continually begged for a dog, but I kept telling them, "We're too busy. The poor dog would be home all day by itself. What about when you both have all your activities?" Those were the exact words my mom told me when I was growing up and wanted a dog.

Well, Bryan changed his mind. He thought having a dog would help motivate him to get out and walk. It would be his "therapy dog." So we started looking for dogs on the Minnesota rescue sites. You could see a little light in his eyes as he looked for puppies. It would be a good thing for him and our family. We needed something else to focus on.

Jenny coordinated another JoasStrong Day. Again people posted pictures on social media wearing their apparel. This time though, Bryan got to participate. We both put on our JoasStrong shirts and posted a picture of us sitting on his hospital bed. During his lunch break and all evening, we watched as people posted their pictures. It was the first time Bryan got a glimpse of all the people who were supporting us. No matter how many times I would tell him, I don't think he comprehended the enormity of it all. Today he did. Every time I would show him a post, he would tear up and silently shake his head from side to side. I would gently put my arm around him and squeeze his shoulder. No words were needed.

One afternoon between therapy sessions, there was a woman standing outside Bryan's room. She was a slender woman with long dark brown hair and a friendly smile. She looked nervous. I had no idea who she was. She motioned to me to come out into the hall.

"Can I help you?" I asked her.

"My name is Betty. I stopped at Bryan's accident scene. I felt I needed to pray over him. So that is what I did. I remained there until the ambulance and police arrived," she explained to me. "I have been following your story since that night. I needed to see Bryan with my own eyes to know that he was OK."

"Oh my goodness," I said, giving her a hug. "You're the one. Others told me there was a woman who prayed over Bryan. Thank you! I would like you to meet Bryan. Come with me."

She followed me into the room. "Bryan, this is Betty. This is the woman who prayed over you at the accident scene."

"Hi, Bryan," Betty said softly, tears filling her eyes. I could see the relief wash over her as she smiled. "I'm so glad to see you are doing well."

Stunned, Bryan replied, "Thank you, Betty. Thank you so much for doing that for me."

"I don't want to take any more of your time, but I had to come and see with my own eyes that you were OK. I will continue to pray for you," she said and then turned to leave.

I walked with her to the elevator and gave her another hug. "Betty, thank you for coming and introducing yourself. It means a lot to both of us."

She stepped on the elevator, and we waved goodbye as the doors closed. The whole interaction was no more than five minutes, but it was a profound moment. Betty got closure on a dire situation that she was a part of, and we got to thank her for surrounding Bryan with the power of prayer from almost the moment of his accident. It's amazing to think that someone was praying for Bryan before I even knew he was in an accident. We were really blessed.

During our time in the ICU, I told myself that, once I knew Bryan was going to be "OK," I was going to get a tattoo. I wanted something permanent that would symbolize this journey. Every time I would see it, I would be reminded of everything we endured, how far we had come, and what was left ahead of us. The word that summarized all of this for me was "BELIEVE"— believe in miracles, believe in the strength of all of us, believe in the good in people, believe we are meant for something more, believe in helping others, believe in not sweating the small stuff, believe in love. I wanted to be able to see it every day, unlike the whale's tail I have on top of my right butt cheek, so I decided to get it on the top of my foot. What made this experience even more special was Erica coming with me. She was going to get a "Believe" tattoo, also.

I dropped Bryan off at his morning therapy and then met Erica at my house. Rockin' Tattoos was located in Eagan. We both had printed out "Believe" in the font of our choice. This was going to be Erica's first tattoo. She was extremely nervous, so she wanted to go first. She handled it like a rockstar. Next, it was my turn. I'm not going to lie; the top of the foot hurt way more than my butt cheek. A flurry of pictures were taken to mark this event.

That night, when I took off the bandage to show Bryan, I was overcome with emotion. Seeing "Believe" forever emblazoned on my foot was confirmation that we had made it through the darkest of our days. Now believe we can look to the future.

Chapter 25

For the Memorial Day weekend, Bryan was given a day pass. We picked Sunday, since that was a therapy-free day. Bryan was going to get to leave the hospital for longer than a wheelchair ride around the block. This was intended for us to go home and try things out. We needed to see if our house was ready for him when it was time to come home.

We waited for the pharmacy to send all of Bryan's necessary daily medications up to the room with instructions for when to administer them. There were only two, so it would be easy. We left the hospital around 10:00 a.m. Wheeling Bryan out to the car was surreal. He was going home, even if it was only for a couple of hours.

Our ride home was very quiet. I couldn't imagine what was going through Bryan's mind. I didn't want to push the chatting too much, instead letting Bryan soak up this experience and his feelings about it. He did say, "North Memorial is really far from home. I wonder why I was flown to that hospital." We later found out it was because, at the time, Dakota County contracted with North Memorial Air Care out of the Lakeville airport (close to the accident scene).

As we turned the corner to our road, we saw that we had a welcome brigade. Shani, Mike, Shelly, Gregg, Elyse, Griffin, my parents, and neighbors lined our cul-de-sac clapping and cheering. Bryan couldn't contain his tears. We hadn't known if this day would ever come, and here we were. Bryan was home. And it was only a few short days until it would be permanent. It was nice to have most of our core group be able to celebrate this moment with us.

As we pulled into the driveway, I had never seen our yard look so stunning. It was as if we had been on the TV show *Extreme Makeover Landscape Edition*. A week before, a group of people (hockey team, some of my students, and their families) had come and done all of our yard work: weeding, planting, and mulching our yard, which was no small feat. We have gardens around our whole house, but none of them had been tended. My neighbors were probably the happiest because they wouldn't have to see all the weeds. *How would I ever be able to thank these people?* Yardwork was the last thing I was thinking about, and yet, these people took it upon themselves to do this—a gift of kindness that keeps on giving.

Metal portable ramps that I had borrowed from a former student who is wheelchair bound were used to get Bryan up the two front steps onto the landing. Our neighbor, John, made a wooden ramp to get from the landing up and over the threshold into the house. He also made a ramp to get from the kitchen down into our sunken living room. All the neighborhood kids (ages six to thirteen) had decorated the wooden ramps with markers. They filled in every possible spot with pictures and words of encouragement—their special gift to us.

The ramps worked. Bryan could get around the whole main level by himself in the wheelchair. Yes, the house was ready.

We tried to make the day low key and not overwhelm Bryan. Once Bryan got situated into the recliner, the kids went and played outside, while the adults took turns hanging out with Bryan in the living room. We had a cookout with hamburgers and brats with all the fixings. This made our day more like a normal day—a perfect way to end our incredible day at home.

We needed to leave the house at 7:00 p.m. to make it back to the hospital by 8:00. It was hard to leave home and go back after getting that little taste of freedom, but knowing that we would be back home for good in a few short days made it easier.

A friend got us a fantastic deal on a sleep number bed that would be delivered to our house the day before we came home. It was recommended that we get that type of bed because it can be adjusted like a hospital bed where the head and foot of the bed can be raised or lowered. Angie came and hung up curtains in the dining room because that was now our makeshift bedroom.

The day before Bryan's release was jam-packed. It started with Dr. Woods, the orthopedic surgeon, coming into the room to give us the results of the previous day's pelvic X-rays. These would determine if Bryan would be able to bear weight on his legs, in other words, stand up. We were very nervous to hear the results.

Dr. Woods began, "Bryan, I am sorry to tell you that the X-rays show that the pelvis is not completely healed. Therefore, you need to remain non-weight-bearing for an additional six weeks. It's healing nicely, but we can't take any chances."

I could tell Bryan was devastated. He put on a brave face, but the look in his eyes was utter sadness. All he could say was, "OK."

He had been hopeful that he would be able to get out of his wheelchair. I tried to be upbeat. "We can do this. What is six more weeks in the grand scheme of things?" *Easy for me to say, since I am not the one in the wheelchair.*

We wanted to thank everyone who was an integral part of our journey and to say goodbye before we left. So next on the agenda was to go back to the ICU, main trauma floor, and therapy area. Since everyone knew Bryan for the Snoopy tattoo on his ankle, we thought maybe a Snoopy memento would be a reminder of the miracle they had been a part of. We knew Hallmark carried a Peanuts keepsake collection, so I sent my mom on a mission to find something appropriate. She had a special knack for finding the perfect card or gift for any occasion. She had an innate sense of remembering events or special occasions and always wanted people to know that they were thought of in a special way.

She texted to tell me, "After going to several stores, I found the perfect gifts. I'll send you pictures."

"Mom, they're perfect," I texted back.

She found some Snoopy figurines. Each statue had a saying on it that reflected our time with each of them. The ICU and main trauma floor received a Snoopy hugging Woodstock with the saying, "Happiness is a hug from the heart." For the rehab floor, it was a Snoopy astronaut with the saying, "The sky's the limit." For the two people who were with us from the beginning, Paul and Becca, we got a Snoopy plaque with the words, "The best days start with your favorite people." As we handed out these gifts, we realized it was not a simple "thank you" but a "thank you for giving Bryan his life back." Tears were shed, and hugs were given.

As we left, Bryan said, "We will be back when I can walk through the doors."

We went back to Bryan's room before he needed to head down to therapy. I gave him a kiss goodbye. "I'll be back in the morning to take you home. Can you even believe it? We are going HOME! Shani will take good care of you tonight." Then I grabbed my purse and keys and ran to my car. I was on my way home to shower. There was so much I needed to do in the next twelve hours.

First, I had to go to school to watch the afternoon kindergarten concert. Many of the students' parents, grandparents, and guests attended to see them perform the spring songs they had learned. I immediately left after they were done singing, missing out on the treats and conversations. I pulled Griffin and Elyse out of school early so we could get to Chippewa Falls for the fundraiser in our hometown that evening.

Nate Plummer, a former day camper of mine and a friend of the family, wanted to put on a concert fundraiser for us. He was living in New York City at the time, auditioning for Broadway, as well as starting his own business, Stage Door Unlocked, which is an online actors training and resource company. Nate's friend, Heidi Joosten, accompanied him. She was a composer, music director/arranger, and a performer in the Chicago area.

The concert was held at The Heyde Center for the Arts, a historic building in Chippewa Falls that was built in 1907 as the Catholic High School. It had been closed for thirty-six years before it was renovated and restored in 2000.

The auditorium was packed with standing room only. It had been years since I had seen many of these people. Seeing our hometown come out in support of us was humbling. People waited to hug me and give me their one-on-one words of encouragement, like a receiving line at a wedding. Nate sang songs from Broadway musicals. For an additional fundraiser, Nate had ten songs listed for people to donate to. The song that raised the most money, he would sing. For the final song, I had requested Nate sing the song "Tomorrow" from Annie. It was the song my mom used every year for the finale of her dance recitals when she taught dance. I never really listened to the words, just did the simple dance she taught me when I was four years old. Now sitting there really listening to the words of the song made me bawl.

When I'm stuck with a day that's gray and lonely,

I just stick up my chin and grin and say.

Oh, the sun will come out tomorrow . . .

Tomorrow, yes tomorrow, Bryan was going to leave the hospital and come home.

After an incredible night of being surrounded by a circle of love, we went back to my parents' home and had a quick snack. I knew I needed to get up early to get back to the hospital, but it wasn't easy to fall asleep. It had been a nonstop day. My mind was racing and reflecting on all the events of the jam-packed day.

But I was also worried about bringing Bryan home. *Is going home going to be a double-edged sword? Am I going to be able to do this? There was no nurses or doctors to help me if things go wrong. Is Bryan really ready to leave? But how good was it going to feel to be home, surrounded by our kids and our own things. We are going to leave our protective bubble and go out into the real world.*

The alarm went off at 4:17 a.m. I got up quietly, trying not to wake the kids who had been sleeping with me. I gently kissed their foreheads. I hastily got dressed and ate a piece of toast before heading out for my two-hour drive back to the hospital.

It was 7:00 a.m. when I arrived at the hospital and took the elevator for the last time up to Bryan's floor. When I walked into his room, there he was, sitting in his wheelchair, dressed and ready to go. We both were full of nervous energy as we waited and waited, which seemed to take forever. We were officially discharged at 11:00 a.m.

Three long months after being admitted, I wheeled Bryan down to the car. He was overcome with emotion that he was finally leaving . . . Going home was what he had been asking for since the ICU. I was crying tears of happiness, relief, and fear. As we waved goodbye to the nurses that walked us down, we closed that chapter of our lives. When the journey started three months earlier, I prayed for this day. It had seemed like an eternity away, but it was finally here. No matter what the future held in store for us, we were going HOME.

Chapter 26

It was our decision that it be a quiet homecoming with just the two of us. It would give us a chance to get settled into our "new" environment. My dad would bring the kids back from Chippewa Falls later that afternoon.

My head was foggy as though I was severely sleep deprived. I had been isolated in the hospital for three months, not having to worry about the day-to-day routine of life. Our world was no longer in the protective bubble of the hospital where my only focus had been Bryan. We had to figure out our new normal. We were home and thrown back into real life taking care of the kids and shuttling them to their summer camps, playdates, band lessons, practices, and games, as well as, cooking, housework, yard work, in addition to the caregiver role for Bryan. Panic was setting in, but good panic. I reminded myself that it was a panic that I could control and handle.

The home nurse came that first night. I needed to learn how to hook Bryan up to his TPN. This needed to be done every night and run for twelve hours. There were so many steps to learn.

1. Get the TPN bag out of the refrigerator one to two hours before to allow it to warm down to room temperature.

2. Once the TPN was at room temperature, I had to mix the TPN with the vitamins.

3. To do that, I needed to clean the top of the vitamin bottle with an alcohol wipe before sticking the needle in to draw up the multivitamin into the syringe.

4. Clean the port on the TPN bag with an alcohol wipe where the vitamins needed to be injected.

5. After I added the vitamins to the TPN, I would mix the injected vitamins by squeezing the bag gently.

6. Hang bag up to allow the TPN to flow down the tubing that would connect to Bryan's PICC line.

7. I would have to inspect the line to make sure there were no bubbles.

8. Put new batteries into the pump. This had to be done each time.

9. Turn the pump on, and put the IV tubing through it.

10. Flush Bryan's PICC line with a saline solution.

11. Use an alcohol wipe to scrub the end of the PICC line and the saline tube.

12. Attach the saline tube to the PICC line.

13. Slowly push the saline into the PICC line.

14. Clean the end of the tubing from the TPN bag, clean the end of Bryan's PICC line again, and then connect.

15. Press the start button.

Holy shit! There was so much to remember. *What if I do something wrong or out of order that hurt Bryan? Other people have done this, right?*

The nurse left after Bryan was all hooked up to the TPN. The nice thing was that the TPN was stored in a backpack, making it portable. This allowed more freedom for Bryan. He could go to the kids' activities, go to the bathroom, or for a walk without dragging an IV pole with him.

The kids had set up their sleeping bags on the floor next to our bed. They wanted to be close. We started watching the movie *Zootopia*, but both Bryan and I were exhausted. It wasn't long before I had to turn the movie off. I told the kids, "We'll finish the movie tomorrow. Dad and I are really tired." They didn't argue.

They took turns hugging and kissing us good night. "It's nice to have you home," Griffin said.

"I'm happy you're home," said Elyse.

Even though we were sleeping in the dining room, we were home. Sleeping in the same bed as my husband, with my kids on the floor next to us, was like a dream. We were all together again, our new beginning.

We still had our meal train. People dropped off dinner for the first few nights we were home and continued three days a week for about a month after—what an extraordinary gift to not have to worry about what to make for dinner on top of everything else.

The next day, the nurse came again. On my own, I had to go through the TPN process one more time while she observed me. I needed to show her that I knew exactly what to do. It was as nerve racking as taking my driver's test. Thankfully, I passed. That was it. Only two times and now I was on really on my own. "Bryan, you can call me Nurse Shauna," I jokingly said.

Nurse Killie, a homecare nurse, was assigned to us and came to the house once a week. Her job was to change the covering on Bryan's PICC line, take a blood sample, check his weight, temperature, heart rate, blood pressure, and oxygen level. It was important that he maintain a weight of one hundred fifty pounds and his vital numbers remain stable. There was no restriction to his diet. He could eat whatever he wanted. He just needed to eat.

Bryan's appetite slowly increased over the next few months as TPN was slowly reduced. They were trying to determine if Bryan could maintain his levels and weight without the TPN as a supplement. They really didn't know if Bryan would ever be able to sustain himself without TPN because of his short gut syndrome. Time would tell.

The Monday morning after we came home, my dad, who had stayed with us for a few days just to make sure I had enough support, did his routine of taking the kids to school, but instead of returning to our house, he headed back to Chippewa Falls. My parents were officially off their three-month "parenting" duty. My security blanket would be an hour-and-a-half away.

Griffin was signed up for a hockey camp that began a week after we got home. The day before camp, he came to me and said, "Mom, I don't think my hockey equipment fits." I had him try it all on, and he was correct. *It figures.* So the first time I left Bryan alone was to go to Play It Again Sports. It was literally right down the road (only three miles away). We bought Griffin a new helmet, chest protector, and elbow pads. We didn't have to get him new skates because, a month earlier, a man from Eagan contacted me. He owned the Saint Mane Sporting Goods store in Minneapolis and wanted to donate a pair of new skates for Griffin. Since outdoor lacrosse would be starting in a few weeks, he also got new lacrosse cleats. Elyse came along too because she needed to get ready for her upcoming volleyball camps, so we purchased a volleyball and two pairs of socks. I wasn't concerned about Bryan for the short time we were gone. He was content to sit in his recliner and watch TV. He promised me that was where he would stay. And he did.

Besides hooking Bryan up to TPN and helping him change his ileostomy bag, he was pretty self-sufficient. He could transfer himself easily in and out of his wheelchair. He could shower himself, only needing help getting his underwear and pants on.

The ileostomy bag changes were something we struggled with. There were so many steps. Bryan had a two-system ileostomy bag: a wafer, which is the seal that goes around the stoma and sticks to the skin, and a bag that is attached to the wafer. The wafer needed to have a hole cut into it to go around the stoma. I would get this pre-cut before the bag change process began. If I cut the hole too big, the stool could leak around the edges and irritate the skin around the stoma. If the hole was cut too small, it could damage the stoma. The bag, which was made of plastic, was about twelve inches long and had an odor-barrier film that contained the odors. At the bottom of the bag was a silicone drain spout that had an attached plug that Bryan opened to allow the stool to come out. His stool would always be liquidy with its consistency ranging from watered-down tomato soup to a Wendy's Frosty depending on what he ate. This was due to Bryan not having a large intestine. The large intestine's job was to absorb liquid from the waste to make it solid.

Bryan would lie in bed on a towel as I laid out all the supplies, kind of like when you get ready to change a diaper. Even though you could be all prepared, you never knew if the baby would start peeing or pooping as the diaper came off or if they tried to crawl away. At least I didn't have to worry about him escaping mid-change.

Once the old bag and wafer were taken off, I needed to go as quickly as possible because we would never know when the stoma would start outputting. The area needed to be cleaned. I was supposed to wipe around the stoma with a skin protectant and then sprinkle an antifungal powder over that. Let that all dry. Sometimes, it would only output a little, and I could wipe it before it touched the prepped skin. But more often than not, if it started outputting, I would have to start the whole prepping process over. There were times that I would spend over an hour wiping and cleaning before I could get the wafer around the stoma and stuck to his skin. Once the wafer was adhered, I just had to attach the bag. That was the easy part. It was like closing a plastic bag by snapping the two ridges together.

We were supposed to change his bag every three to four days, but there were many times that the bag would leak, come unsnapped, or the wafer would come unsealed from his skin. When this happened, there would be stool everywhere. It was not a fun 2:00 a.m. wake-up call. While Bryan would shower, I would change the bedding and get the dirty sheets into the washing machine. Then I would get all my supplies ready for a new bag. At times it was so frustrating that I wanted to give up, but that wasn't an option because Bryan's life depended on it. Eventually I got better at it, and down the road, after many attempts, Bryan learned to do it on his own. He figured out that the best time to do a bag change was in the morning before he had anything to eat or drink because the output was minimal.

I tried to take Bryan for a short walk every day to let him get some fresh air. He didn't love being pushed around the neighborhood in his wheelchair, but too bad; he needed it. We would go to Griffin's lacrosse games. Pushing a wheelchair through grass to get to the field wasn't a smooth ride. The wheels would get caught in the long grass, or we would hit a bump causing me to almost dump him a few times.

Bryan and I continued to look for puppies. The kids were beyond excited. We headed to PetSmart one Sunday afternoon because they were having a pet adoption day through Wags and Whiskers Rescue. The first dog we saw was an adorable brindle puppy named Stella. The kids and I loved her, but Bryan wasn't totally sure. He wasn't one for making quick decisions. He didn't want to sell ourselves short and not look around more. We went around to the other dogs. Most were over two years old and didn't pique our interests. Before we left, I filled out paperwork on Stella to do a meet and greet with her, which was the first step in the adoption process. Stella's foster mom brought her to our house the next week. The person she had to win over was Bryan, and he fell hook, line, and sinker for her. We filed the paperwork to officially adopt her. It was a little sooner than I wanted. Bryan still being wheelchair-bound meant the training was going to fall solely on me. Not ideal, but seeing the joy it was bringing to the kids and Bryan, I couldn't say no.

We had to get ready for a puppy. We liked the name Stella but wanted to choose our own name. After much deliberation, we decided on Willow. It was the name of the street Bryan and I grew up on. It was a fun day at the pet store. The kids were running around the store wanting to buy everything in it. They loved picking the collar, leash, dishes, bed, treats, and toys. The last thing was to make the nametag.

"Are we all sure of the name Willow?" I asked.

"Yes," Bryan, Griffin, and Elyse all answered in unison.

On June 23, Willow officially became a part of the Joas family. Her adoption was one of the best things we could have done. Willow helped us shift the focus off the accident. We were all in puppy heaven.

Chapter 27

We anxiously awaited Bryan's appointment for his pelvic X-ray on July 6. I didn't know how much more patience Bryan had left being in a wheelchair. I felt confident that his pelvis would be ready, but there was always a sliver of doubt. Waiting for the doctor to come in was torture. Finally, the door opened. "Your pelvis is healed."

Bryan broke down. He had been waiting so long for those words. They had him stand right then. He was very wobbly and shaky, like watching a toddler stand for the first time. But this was literally one step on the path to "normal."

He would need to walk with crutches or my grandpa Ralph's walker. Bryan's tree-trunk biker thighs were now the size of toothpicks. The first thing he made me do when we got home was pack up the wheelchair. "I'm done with that!" he proudly announced. Finally, some of the control of the recovery was going on to Bryan's shoulders. He was mobile and able to get stronger without being dependent on me or other medical professionals to make the progress.

Getting rid of the wheelchair motivated Bryan more. It is amazing what people can accomplish with a little motivation. He progressed quickly from that point. He was weak and had pain getting into motion again, but there was no longer anyone telling him what he could not do physically. He started doing a lot of movement, first just the ability to get up and down, to navigating with a walker or crutches. Fifteen days after he was given the OK to stand, he stopped using any assistance to walk. The kids and I were swimming at the neighbor's pool, which was six houses down. It was a hot summer day. The kids were having fun jumping in and playing with their friends. Out of the corner of my eye, I spotted Bryan standing by the fence. I wasn't surprised to see him there, but then I noticed he was missing something important.

"Where are your crutches?" I shouted.

"I didn't use them," he casually replied.

"What?" I stammered. "You could have fallen. That was so dumb."

"I'm done with them," he calmly answered.

I knew I wasn't going to change his mind. That had been Bryan's attitude on many things over the years; there was no reason to make a big deal out of something that was expected. He felt he was stable enough to walk and had the confidence to do it, although he looked awfully shaky as we walked back home, which made me nervous that he might fall. He used a slow shuffle process to walk. You could see the effort was taking a lot of his energy as he had no stamina for any physical activity. He powered through that 100-yard walk, and I knew he would never use those crutches again.

THEN, three days after he walked without crutches, which I was getting used to, he rode his bike around the neighborhood. Of course, he kept this news from me as I would not have been very pleased if he would have asked for permission. His comment after was "It feels so much better than walking." I gave in and thought I better capture this on video.

I tried not to show my fear because I knew there was no stopping him now.

"Biking is no more dangerous for me than walking. I have better control on my bike."

I think that is a skewed opinion, but who am I to argue with this? It was like letting your kids do things for the first time. Yes, you are fearful, but you still let them go.

Summer was filled with healing, family time, and training Willow. Now that Bryan was able to walk, he insisted we move back upstairs to our bedroom. He wanted to sleep in our old bed and not have to shower in the kitchen.

Bryan's next step was to start his path back to full time work by easing into it a few hours a day starting in mid-July. We were definitely working toward our life resembling a pre-accident normal. We got back into the routine of life. It was a little different, but we'd take it.

Chapter 28

There were a few things on our list that we wanted to do before school started and Bryan went back to work full time. The first thing was to have Bryan meet Tony and Alexa. I had promised them that, when Bryan was better, they would get to meet him. He needed to meet his angels.

We decided to meet at a restaurant that was halfway between our houses. It was a bar and grill, so the atmosphere would be more relaxed. I could only imagine the anxiety Bryan, Alexa, and Tony would feel meeting each other. The last time they "saw" each other was in a dire situation that Bryan couldn't even remember.

At first we talked about everything but the accident. Alexa made little eye contact with Bryan, stealing quick glances. I am sure the image of Bryan at the accident scene was flashing through her mind.

It was only after dinner that our conversation turned toward the accident. I asked Tony and Alexa if they would tell Bryan their side of the story. So, they proceeded to take turns telling the story they had told me. Bryan sat in silence, tears welling up in his eyes a few times.

"When the paramedics told you that they were going to have to cut off your biking jersey," Tony said, smiling, "you made it clear that you were not happy about it. The paramedics told you, 'I'm sorry; I know these are expensive.' You replied, 'It's new.'"

I had to smile. It was a new long-sleeved jersey that Gregg had given him a few months earlier. It was incredible that, even though Bryan had no recollection of the accident, he had been awake at the scene.

It was therapeutic for Bryan to hear the story directly from them. It was a story that only they could tell him. It was a healing night not only for Bryan, but for Tony and Alexa as well.

"I don't know how to thank you," Bryan told them. "You saved my life."

"We were just at the right place at the right time," Tony replied.

"When you are in the medical field, you automatically do what you have been trained to do to save a life," Alexa stated. "I'm glad God put me there to help."

After hugging them goodbye, we knew that Alexa and Tony would forever be connected to us.

The second thing on our list was to pick up Bryan's bike, helmet, and bike clothes from the sheriff's office. Bryan wanted to see everything. He was still trying to piece together how this could have happened. The lead investigator, Ryan, had pictures from the accident scene, and they pulled up all the evidence on the screen in a conference room.

There were pictures of the emergency vehicles at the scene and the helicopter right on the road. The road Bryan was riding on was a perfect biking road. There were wide shoulders, small rolling hills, and minimal traffic. It was unfathomable seeing the photos of how it could have happened. They pointed out where Bryan's bike was found and where he was found, three hundred yards away. There were no skid marks to help them reenact the scene. In addition to hardly any evidence, there were no eyewitnesses and no video footage. Still, the whole Dakota County sheriff's office was astonished that someone still wasn't caught. They tried to offer apologies, but we wouldn't let them. There was nothing they could have done differently.

The bike was the last thing they gave us. I gasped and placed my hand over my mouth in utter horror. The back of the bike frame was dangling and only hanging by the rear brake cable. The back wheel rim was broken and bent inward toward the middle of the wheel. The seat was turned sideways. The impact Bryan must have endured was more than an accidental bump off the road. You could see exactly where the vehicle hit. It made me sick to my stomach. *How can this be Bryan's bike? It's hard to believe he survived.* I tried not to envision Bryan being hit and then being thrown off his bike into the ditch. *How can a person do that and drive away?*

Bryan sadly shook his head. "Oh my God. Oh my God. What a mess."

We took the bike and put it in the van to drive home. On the way home, Bryan started analyzing the damage to the bike and tried to determine just what happened. That was the way Bryan's logical mind worked. "When I look at the damage to the bike, I think I rode on top of the hood of the vehicle before I got flung off."

The last thing we wanted to do was go back to North Memorial to say "Hi" and "Thank you." We gave each floor Bryan had been on, along with Becca and Paul, containers of mint treats with a note that said, "Thank you for your commit-'mint.' These are for your enjoy-'mint.'" It was nice to show everyone what their hard work and dedication could do, especially on the ICU floor. It isn't very often they get to see the end result.

Chapter 29

Bryan started back to work full time on September 1, while the rest of us were back to school a few days later. It was crazy. *How can we be back to our normal routine six months after such a horrific accident?* Multiple times a day, I stopped and marveled at it—the miracle.

Then came the JoasStrong FUNdraiser. From the beginning of our journey, Shani, Jenny, Angie, Carmen, and Jaleh had a goal of hosting a fundraiser to help us financially with costs now and in the future. They wanted it to be a kid-friendly event with face painting and temporary tattoos. It had been planned for late September at Carbone's Pizza & Pub in Rosemount. The manager, Cynthia, was such a gracious member of the community, and she was more than willing to help out with the event.

The committee had met about once a month and had a Google spreadsheet that tracked all the incoming silent-auction items they each acquired. The ladies left me out of the planning. They wanted me to sit back, enjoy the night, and not worry about anything. It meant so much for me to see my friends from different circles join together in this effort for us.

There were ninety-nine generously donated items, such as Packer tickets, Vikings tickets, an autographed Wisconsin Badger basketball, restaurant gift cards, quilts, and various baskets (chocolate, wine, lottery, etc.), which were used for silent-auction items, prizes for drawings, and mystery bags. They filled the whole back room of Carbone's. These donations came from friends, acquaintances, and even strangers.

Bryan's childhood friend offered his band, Bigly, to provide the entertainment. They played a wide range of music to accommodate all the guests, including the kids. By the end of the night, the dance floor was packed with people having a blast.

The turnout was overwhelming. You have the best intentions of talking to all the guests, but the time goes so quickly, that goal is not met. It was nice to thank as many people as we could, face to face, for all of their support.

It was the first time most people had seen Bryan since the accident. There were many happy tears shed for the "miracle man." It was nice for people to see him and give him a hug. Bryan hated to be the center of attention, but he definitely was the man of the night. We had the tangled mess of his bike on display. It was a shocking visual for people to witness. There were lots of gasps and comments: "I can't believe he survived" and "It doesn't even look like a bike."

We were fortunate enough to have had many smaller fundraisers done for us throughout our journey. These included a lemonade stand, a neighborhood garage sale, handmade bracelets and keychain sale, as well as two local restaurants (McDonalds and Granite City) having a JoasStrong Night. The Eagan Hockey Association had a root beer float night with a silent auction. All of these acts of kindness reminded us how people, many of them strangers, supported us and wished us well. For almost all of those fundraisers, Bryan had been in the hospital, so it was just the kids and me who were able to attend. Those had been more somber with the words, "We're praying for you," "Stay strong," and "Bryan is a fighter," but this one was different. Bryan was there. People got to see him, hug him, talk with him, and laugh with him. They were no longer reading about his journey on CaringBridge but actually standing there witnessing a miracle—Bryan. For many, their prayers were answered. Yes, it was a fundraiser, but it really turned into a huge celebration of family, friends, and faith. At this event, Bryan and his friends started planning their next adventure. Mike had lined up a deal with Spring Street Sports to get fat bikes for him, Gregg, and Bryan. Bryan was also planning on how to get back to the gravel races and rides they were starting to do more of.

Chapter 30

Bryan and I were trying to think of ways to say thank you to my parents. They stopped their lives to take care of Griffin and Elyse without thinking twice. They gave up their fiftieth anniversary dream trip. We would be forever grateful. I knew they wanted no thanks and would never expect anything. Over and over my mom said, "It is what parents are supposed to do. You need to be there for your kids no matter what."

I was searching on the *Today Show* or the *Ellen Show* for a fun way that we could honor them. I mean, how cool would it be to be on one of those shows. I submitted to "One Million Acts of Good" on the *Ellen Show* and "Everyone Has a Story" on the Kathie Lee and Hoda portion of the *Today Show*. The chances were unlikely, but why not try, right? Well, right before Labor Day, I got an email from Madison at the *Today Show*. They read my submission for "Everybody Has a Story" and they would love to consider us. HOLY SHIT! My letter was actually read. I couldn't believe it. I told Bryan and Erica right away.

"Would you mind revising your submission letter so it has more details," Madison wrote, "especially about how much your parents and their generosity means to your family? Aim for around three hundred words, please."

My mom loves Hoda. This would be the ultimate "thank you." So Bryan and I got to work, rewriting. I also enlisted the help of Erica. Changes were made, and details were added. The three of us felt it was ready to be sent:

On the night of March 8, 2016, my husband, Bryan, was riding his bicycle home from work, when someone hit him and left the scene. He was airlifted to a hospital forty-five minutes from our home, where he was admitted to the ICU. He had internal bleeding and a broken pelvis and back. At the time of the accident, my parents were driving from Wisconsin to Florida, where they had rented a condo for a month. They were in Nashville when I had to make the dreaded call. They immediately offered to help, turned around, and drove to our house in Minnesota to help care for our two children, eight and ten years old. Bryan was in the ICU for six weeks and underwent multiple surgeries, procedures, and dialysis. The road to recovery was very uncertain. With the hospital being so far away, I could not commute back and forth every day. My parents offered to stay as long as they needed to. This allowed me to stay with Bryan twenty-four-seven. They took the kids to school, all of their after-school activities, helped the kids with homework, and comforted them when needed. Our son, Griffin, said it best: "Meme and Papa took me and my sister to school a little late (the first day back). After that day, it felt pretty normal." As the weeks went on, my mom told me, "You need to be with Bryan; we have the kids." I knew that my kids were being taken care of as well as or even better than if I was there. This allowed me to concentrate on caring for Bryan. I continued to be with Bryan through his entire three-month hospital stay. My parents put their life on hold until Bryan was luckily able to come home from the hospital. There is no real way to thank them or acknowledge how much we appreciated all they did. They symbolize the true meaning of family and the sacrifices parents make for their children.

I hadn't told anyone else about this. I didn't want to until I knew it was a sure thing. Finally a month later, I got an email back that said, "Kathie Lee wants to have you guys on in November." I was going to be able to thank my parents in a one-of-a-kind way.

Holy moly, we were going to be on the *Today Show* with Kathie Lee and Hoda. I couldn't believe I had to keep this secret from my parents for two months! But finally it was time to tell my parents.

It was difficult to get everyone organized. I was in the middle of parent-teacher conferences. On our first attempt, Erica left school at lunchtime. The school she taught at was only two blocks from my parents' house. I wanted Erica to video me FaceTime my parents. However, my mom was at the dentist's.

Erica called the dentist's to have them tell her to "come right home and not stop for any errands. Shauna has something to tell her. Tell her NOTHING IS WRONG."

The bad news was they didn't tell her the part about nothing being wrong, so she cried all the way home thinking the worst—something happened to Bryan or the kids, I would tell her that I had cancer, etc. When she got home, she ran into the house hysterical. "What's wrong? What happened? Erica, why are you here?"

"There is nothing wrong!" Erica said, giving her a hug. "What Shauna has to tell us is good news. I promise."

"So you know what it is?" my dad asked Erica.

"I do, but I was sworn to secrecy. Shauna needs to tell you. I have to get back to school, but I'll be back at 5:00 p.m. That is when she has her next break."

Five o'clock finally came. Erica texted me that she was ready to video them. As I made the Facetime call, my heart was pounding.

"Are you ready?" I asked my parents.

"Yes. We have been waiting all day," they both answered in unison.

"I nominated you to be on the Kathie Lee and Hoda show, and WE WERE CHOSEN!" I burst out.

"WHAT?" they both said, mouths hanging open and eyes wide.

"We are going to New York to be on the show!" I continued.

"For what? Why would they have us on?" my mom questioned.

"We wanted to find a way to thank you. We told them our story, and the rest is history," I said.

"You've got to be kidding," my dad said.

"They want us to be on the November 17 segment, where they sing—" I started to say.

My mom interrupted, "I love that segment. Kathie Lee writes a song. It's called 'Everyone Has a Story.'"

"But this time, the song will be for you," I continued.

"Oh my God. I can't believe this," my mom said, crying. "This can't be real."

"It's real," I reassured her.

"This is awesome! I love Hoda and Kathie Lee. I can't believe we are going to meet them," she rambled.

"I told you it was nothing bad."

Then my mom's excitement turned to panic. "BUT I don't fly. How am I going to get there?"

"Don't worry. That's taken care of. I told them that you don't fly, so they are making arrangements for you to take Amtrak. Some of the details still need to be finalized, but we are going. Now we have to get ready!" I explained.

"This is certainly good news. Never in my dreams would I have thought you were going to tell us this," my dad said.

"My parent-teacher conference starts in one minute, so I really have to run. I love you. I will call you later. New York, here we come!"

In the next two weeks, I had to get outfits ready for all of us for the show, get a substitute for my class, and submit pictures of my parents and our family. They were going to use the photos to make a video to play at the beginning of the segment.

Erica, Morgan, and Ingrid decided to come to New York City, too. We would make it a long weekend and take in the sights together as a family.

When Bryan, Elyse, Griffin, and I arrived at JFK airport, a chauffeured town car sent by NBC was waiting to pick us up and take us to our hotel across from Rockefeller Center. Driving through the busy streets of NYC, I felt like a celebrity.

After settling in, we walked to Times Square and had pizza at Carmine's. It had been a long day, so we headed back to the hotel for the night.

The next morning, I met with Rekha, an intern for the *Today Show*, at Rockefeller Center. She took me upstairs to the recording studio. I went into a small booth. There were headphones there for me to put on. Rekha showed me the button to push when I was ready. They needed a recording of me reading the essay I had submitted to be on the show. This audio would be played over the video they had made with all the family photos.

Later, we all gathered in the lobby of our hotel where Rekha met us to walk us over to the studio. My mom and I would be getting our hair and makeup done. I had never had that done before, not even for my wedding.

While getting my hair done, Isla Fisher came out of the changing room. She was on the *Today Show* during the 9 to 10 a.m. hour, promoting her movie *Nocturnal Animals*. The Broadway singer, Lora Lee Gayer, who was going to be singing our song, was right next to me getting her hair and makeup done, as well. Kathie Lee came in to welcome us. We still had a while to wait until it was our turn to go upstairs. Our family sat in the green room with Tate Donovan who sat scrolling through his phone. He was there promoting his movie *Manchester By the Sea*. We tried to act like sitting with all of these celebrities was totally natural, even though we were in awe of all that was happening and the people we were seeing.

Finally, it was our time. We were going to be on right after "Ambush Makeover." Stepping onto the set was like entering another world. There were so many lights and cameras. The set was much smaller than I imagined it would be. It is truly amazing how big they make it seem on TV. Kathie Lee and Hoda were very gracious and down to earth. Rekha told us that it would all go very quickly. She wasn't kidding. It was over before I even had time to think about it. So much happened in such a little amount of time.

The show started with Bryan and me, along with my parents, sitting on the couch with Hoda and Kathie Lee. Erica and the kids were off to the side watching. They opened the show with the video of our story. To see and hear what they had produced as the introduction to our story was so overwhelming. It was hard to comprehend it. It didn't help that we were surrounded by TVs, cameras, and lights. I wanted to burst into tears but couldn't. I was "live" on national TV. I didn't want to make a fool of myself by crying, snorting, or blowing my nose. I sat like a mannequin with a smile on my face as I tried to block it all out.

When the video was over, Hoda and Kathie Lee asked questions of each one of us. We were not told what questions would be asked. It was all off the cuff. Knowing this was being broadcast on national television made it all the more nerve wracking.

During one of the commercial breaks, Hoda reached over and asked, "Did they catch the person that did this to you?"

Bryan said, "No."

Hoda said, "Really? REALLY?" shaking her head.

Kathie Lee raised her pointer finger and said, "But, God knows, someday that person will have to answer to Him."

Hoda invited Griffin and Elyse over to the couches when Lora Lee sang the song to us. Kathie Lee had taken the line, "Road to Recovery," out of my submitted entry and that became the title of the song Lora Lee sung. The words of the song embodied the journey we had been on:

During our darkest and deepest night.

We finally see the light through the rain.

On the hardest of roads we'll ever know.

The road to recovery. The long road to home.

At the end of the show, Erica, Morgan, and Ingrid joined us on the couches. Kathie Lee and Hoda gave us all tickets to "The Ride," an interactive bus tour of the city, and tickets to the Broadway show "Holiday Inn" that Lora Lee was starring in.

After the show ended, we got a quick picture of all of us. Kathie Lee and Hoda gave us all hugs and thanked us for coming. Then they were off to do some taping for the next day's show. We went back to the green room to gather our things and head back to our hotel.

We had just enough time to change our clothes and have a bite to eat before we needed to board "The Ride." When we got on the bus, all the seats were facing the left side of the bus, with two rows of stadium seating. There were floor-to-ceiling windows as well as a glass roof, allowing a full view as we toured the city. We had two hosts, one at each end of the bus, who were comedians. They kept us entertained and laughing the whole trip. Actors were strategically placed along the route, unbeknownst to people on the streets, to perform for us. For example, in Columbus Circle, a ballerina and her partner danced to "Christmas Eve/Sarajevo." It was a unique and fun way to see the sights of downtown NYC.

The next few days, we were on our own. It was like a whirlwind. We tried to see and do as much as we could. The highlights were seeing the Rockefeller tree as it was being decorated for Christmas, going to the Rockettes Christmas Spectacular, riding the subway to Battery Park to see the Statue of Liberty, making the trek to the 9/11 Memorial, and then to Central Park.

Walking was our means of getting around. Even though Bryan was still working on his endurance, he was determined to keep up with us. My mom was happy to have a "slow-walking" companion. The only thing he couldn't do was skate with us. "Even though I wasn't able to skate with you, watching all of you on the Rockefeller Center Rink was a thrill and a little bittersweet," Bryan told me later.

The tickets for "Holiday Inn" were for our last night in NYC. Our seats were in the front row of the balcony. About twenty minutes before the show started, I received a Facebook message from Lora Lee that said, "Excited you guys are here tonight! If you wait in the house, I will come out and say hello after the show."

The show was phenomenal with a mixture of singing and incredible tap dancing. It lived up to the reputation that Hoda and Kathie Lee raved about. After the show, Lora Lee introduced us to all of her costars, one of them being Corbin Bleu. My nieces were huge fans of him because he was a star in the Disney movie *High School Musical*. They were ecstatic to get a picture with him. Lora Lee told her fellow cast members that we were the family she had sung for and why. They were all so kind when they came to meet us. It was the ultimate way to end the trip.

EPILOGUE

March 8, 2016, marks the day of our life-altering traumatic event. We are not the same as we were, nor will we ever be. "Life can change in an instant," so the saying goes. I used to blow it off and not seriously think about it. It wouldn't happen to us, I thought. But it did happen. In an instant, we ended up on an extreme roller coaster ride, with hills touching the sky and drops going to the center of earth. Slowly, ever so slowly, the hills, the drops, and the inversions became less intense as we came to the rolling hills at the end of the ride.

When you look death in the face, you figure out the things that really matter and learn to prioritize. This experience made us slow down and see things with new eyes. The relationship between Bryan and me has grown stronger, but that doesn't mean we don't experience the typical married couple spats. We are human, but now we appreciate each other more. We try to not take each other for granted and enjoy just being together: taking Willow on walks, running errands, attending our kids' sporting events, or just sitting in the same room.

The kids have been on their own roller coaster. We tried to shelter them from all the "medical stuff." We were so fortunate to have their Meme and Papa substituting for us and keeping things as normal as possible. This meant getting them to and from school, taking them to their extracurricular activities, setting up playdates, and allowing the neighborhood kids to play on the trampoline or go in the basement to play hockey. I don't know how I would have done it without them. The kids felt comfortable with my parents, so it was a fairly easy adjustment. When Bryan and I finally came home, it signaled that all was OK. Our schedules were as hectic as ever. The kids learned to adjust to Dad being in a wheelchair when he first came home and taking extra care to help out with the little things, like refilling his water glass, getting his medicine, helping set up the ramps, etc. We were all under the same roof, and that was what mattered.

Many people in the medical field who were following our story now tell us, "I never thought Bryan would make it." He truly is a miracle. The doctors who worked tirelessly to keep him alive, along with Bryan's own strength and self-determination, got him through. Once he was told he wasn't sick any more, his healing went into fast-forward. If you didn't know it, you would never believe that Bryan was on the brink of death multiple times. On the outside, he is a healthy, active fifty-year-old dad who is back to work full time, riding his bike, and coaching Griffin's lacrosse team.

However, there are things that will never be the same. Bryan has been completely off TPN since October 2016 and has been able to sustain his weight on his own. Since food and drinks pass through him so quickly, he can eat anything and everything with no restrictions. I soon realized that I had to stop trying to keep up with him, because my waistline did NOT stay the same. Bryan can also dehydrate quickly, since the main purpose of the large intestine, which was completely removed, is to absorb water and salts from the undigested food. This has a direct effect on his kidneys, and he has been labeled with chronic kidney disease. This is something his doctor closely monitors, with blood work every three months. Eventually, this may mean dialysis again or even a kidney transplant. We will conquer that if or when that happens.

Not only was Bryan's kidney function compromised owing to the damage they endured in the accident, so was his liver. He has to strictly limit any alcohol consumption and is prohibited from taking any pain medication, except with a doctor's permission. No ibuprofen or aspirin can be taken for a headache or body aches like most people do. He also is deficient in iron, vitamin B, and vitamin D. I give him a vitamin B injection every month, and he takes iron and vitamin D supplements daily to try to regulate those.

His ileostomy bag is a lifetime consequence Bryan has to deal with. There are lots of products out there to help. Bryan wears a hernia belt all the time. This stiff elastic belt is eight inches wide. Not only does the belt hold his abdominal hernia in place, it has a hole in it to allow the ileostomy bag to come through and puts some pressure on the seal of the bag to keep it extra secure. It reminds me of a corset. To help prevent chafing and ease the discomfort from the belt, he wears a t-shirt underneath. He had to cut a hole in the side to allow his bag to come through. He also wears a Lycra band around his stomach that has a pocket for holding the bag so it doesn't dangle. Once he figured out his system, this has helped with the bag leaks. It's one thing to be at home when the bag leaks; it's another thing being at work, on your bike, or out in public. You can only imagine the mess. Bryan constantly touches his bag to check if it is filled. He has to be careful of the bag getting too full; otherwise, the bag can leak or, worse yet, rip off his skin. When he says, "I need to find a bathroom," that means NOW. It can present some frustration to him and to our family. When we are away from home, he has to be cognizant of where the bathrooms are at all times because he never knows when the bag will be full. He has the added discomfort of having to use a stall versus a urinal. If the stall is in use, there is the added anxiety of having to wait.

The one positive thing about his ileostomy bag is that he doesn't have the excuse to disappear and go sit on the toilet for an hour "going to the bathroom." He even can crack a joke about his situation. One time when my parents were visiting, my dad came out of the bathroom and said, "Who didn't flush the toilet? There is a big turd in there!"

"It wasn't me," Bryan snickered with a sly smile on his face.

Bryan says there are two things that really bother him: his feet and his abdominal hernia. The accident caused him to have neuropathy in his feet, which makes them extremely sensitive. They are numb, like when your feet get really cold, and they feel tingly when you touch them. They also cramp up a lot. Even a slight bump to his feet causes him severe pain. He found that wearing socks all the time helps alleviate some of the pain.

He hates his abdominal hernia. "It's like having a beer belly that you can't get rid of. It gets in the way and makes maintaining the ileostomy harder." Wearing a stiff girdle, twenty-four seven, to hold it in is uncomfortable in more ways than one. If you were to look at the hernia, it is only covered by a thin skin graft, so you can actually see the food moving through the small intestine he has left. It makes a gurgling sound as it is being pushed through that is audible to anyone near him. Plus, if there is a big burst of output into the ileostomy bag, it can make an embarrassing sound, like a fart that he can't control.

In December 2016, nine months after the accident, we finally got to meet with the GI surgeon at the University of Minnesota. Being a fellow cyclist, he was not happy to hear that someone did this to Bryan. Unfortunately, he said without a doubt "no" to reversing the ileostomy and fixing the hernia. There were so many valid reasons why.

1. It would be way too risky.

2. Bryan can't lose any more of his intestines, so if it doesn't work, there is nothing extra to work with.

3. He would have constant diarrhea, which would hinder him from doing any activities. The diarrhea would destroy his rectum.

4. Bryan doesn't have enough rectal stump left to connect to.

5. As for the hernia, everything was working perfectly. To try and close
    it up would risk his intestines getting twisted or pinched. Again, he
    had no extra intestine to fall back on, so we couldn't take the risk.

It was devastating to hear. Looking at Bryan's face broke my heart. He so wanted this, and now all that hope was gone. But listening to the GI surgeon's explanation made it easy to be able to close that window of hope. Bryan's life would actually be more "normal" with the bag. We accepted the decision and were at peace with it.

Bryan's body doesn't work the same way it used to. He can't go as far or as fast as he used to on his bike. I have to remind him, "Bryan, you are on your bike. It doesn't matter." It takes his body a lot longer to recover. He used to be able to go sixty miles on his bike without much of an afterthought. Now, if he rides more than thirty miles, it takes him days to recuperate enough to get back to normal. The accident has aged him. He wouldn't be happy with me saying that, but he doesn't move with as much agility as he did before. Bryan feels like his body is weak overall. His strength hasn't come back to what it was before the accident, and he doesn't know if it ever will. If he lies down on the floor to stretch, watch TV, or play with the dog, getting up is a painstaking event. There are lots of aches and pains that weren't there before. He lost three inches of height and is now slightly hunched forward owing to the break in his back.

Intimacy is not without issues. Bryan had a difficult time getting over the bag hanging from his body. "There's a bag of shit hanging off of me," he would say. "How romantic." Things don't work the same since his pelvis was crushed. We figured it out. We have discovered that it doesn't have to be only the physical act, but a look or touch can be just as intimate.

While I was in the midst of the hospital ordeal, I didn't have time to think. My body and mind were on automatic pilot. Once my caretaker role subsided and Bryan didn't need my full attention, my mind was able to start processing what really happened. My anxiety steadily increased with continuous thoughts of how this trauma was going to affect my family now and in the future. As the one-year anniversary of the accident was approaching, it came to a point that I knew I needed to go to therapy. It was necessary to make sure I had processed everything and to obtain strategies to have on hand if any issues would arise in the future. Dealing with survivor's guilt was one of the hardest issues for me and still is. There are people all over the world who pray for miracles to happen. Why were we picked to receive a miracle? How did we win the lottery on miracles? There has to be a reason we were chosen. I don't know what it is yet, but there is something Bryan or I are meant to do.

Dealing with the disappointment from the lack of support from Bryan's family was something that came out in therapy. It surprised me that it had affected me so deeply. I thought we had a good relationship, but throughout this ordeal, the things that were said and done were so hurtful. My therapist gave me this visual that really resonated with me. "Picture a target. You are in the center with a small circle around you. People in that circle are your direct support. They were there for you consistently. Think about who is in that inner circle for you. Now move to the next circle. Those are the people that assisted you from a distance: they sent you cards, wrote on CaringBridge, let you know they thought of you. Move to the last circle. This consists of people who are your acquaintances. They know you and you know them, but that is about the extent of it. It is OK if Bryan's family is not in that inner circle for you. Being thrown into a dire situation like you were, people showed their true colors. It is not uncommon to feel the way you do. Continue to rely on your inner circles."

When I stopped to think about the people in each circle, I discovered my inner circle was huge. It was who I relied on to get me through, who helped me up when I couldn't stand on my own, and who will continue to be my support. Today, my inner circle is still filled with my rocks, and it is my intention to be in their inner circle. Mike's words echo in my head: "I will hold you up."

We are now six years out from the accident, and Bryan hasn't gone to therapy. I haven't seen any signs of PTSD. I am sure that Bryan not remembering any of the accident or the following six weeks plays a considerable role in that. He can go biking with no fear. We do have some new gadgets in place to help my unease. We have two apps that track him: Life360 and Strava. That was one of the biggest factors that prevented me from calling the police back then. I had no idea where he went biking. Bryan added daytime front and back lights to increase visibility. His most recent gadget is the Garmin Varia, which is a radar that detects cars approaching from behind. The radar is connected to the bike computer Bryan has on his handlebars. A dot on the computer represents a car approaching and shows it moving closer until it passes by. The radar also has a light that is visible to the driver from a mile away and will change its blink pattern to draw more attention to the rider. Even with all the added safety measures, I still have that twinge of anxiety every time he goes on a bike ride. It has gotten better since the first time he went on a solo ride. I watched "the dot" on the GPS tracker from the beginning of the ride to the end and was ready to call 911 if "the dot" stopped for more than a regular traffic stop.

I, on the other hand, haven't liked to bike on the road by myself since the accident. The trauma of that night, starting with not knowing where Bryan was, to the knock on the door, to all the surgeries, complications, and the unknowns that followed makes biking for me too overwhelming and anxiety ridden. My triathlon days went on a hiatus. It was hard to train when I only stuck to spin class or bike paths. Even on the paths, I am hesitant. When I cross an intersection, I check left, right, left, right, and continue to check for cars like my head is a windshield wiper until I am on the other side of the road, whether I am biking, walking, or running. My friends finally convinced me to do a team triathlon with them five years post-accident. I did the running part. Being surrounded by the energy and excitement of the triathletes got me thinking: maybe I could compete again. So, almost seven years after the accident, I signed up for my first individual triathlon. It was thrilling and terrifying all at the same time.

We never know when the trauma of the accident is going to rear its ugly head and reignite many of those same emotions for our family. My children's childhood innocence was taken away. They learned a hard lesson too early that bad things can and do happen. Three-and-a-half years after Bryan's accident, a neighborhood friend and hockey teammate of Griffin's was hit while he was biking to school. He died shortly after. It had been Patric's thirteenth birthday. For me, survivor's guilt came back with a vengeance. *Why did Bryan get to live while Patric died? How can I look at Patric's parents and not feel guilty?*

For Bryan, Patric's death was a shock. He was devastated at the thought that this could have been easily his family mourning the loss of him. Being that Patric was on a bike did not lessen or worsen the tragedy. Bryan wrote the following in the card we gave Patric's family:

> I don't have the emotional fortitude to verbally tell you this, so I am putting it in a letter. I wanted to let you know that, based on my experience, Patric's last memories were of his family, birthday, seeing friends at school, and practice later in the day. As violent and brutal as the accident looked to everyone else, for him, I can honestly say and believe it was not felt the same way. The human body is amazing at going into shock and not letting our minds process things while we are in that moment. I hope this helps you have peace of mind about the accident. As horrible as it was, it is not the same for the victim as all observers of it. Patric was an amazing kid, and I enjoyed every minute that I had the opportunity to coach and watch him grow. He will always be in my memory and thoughts.

The first thing that Griffin asked me about Patric's accident was, "Did the driver stop? Was Patric all alone?" The driver not stopping for Bryan was something that Griffin couldn't understand. After Bryan's accident, he would say, "How could someone drive away from my dad and leave him there?" Those are questions he will ask for the rest of his life.

After Patric's death, the school offered counseling to a group of kids that the staff had identified. Griffin was one of those kids. They brought in an outside counselor, once a week, to meet with the group of eight to ten kids. I think it helped Griffin work through what happened to Patric but also deal with some repressed emotions he didn't even know he had from Bryan's accident.

Neither Bryan nor I have been angry at the driver that hit him. It wouldn't have changed what Bryan went through. We couldn't waste any energy on that aspect of the accident. Detective Fitzgerald called to tell me that they were closing Bryan's case, seven months after the accident. "We are closing the case because there have been no new leads for months. Just because we are closing the case doesn't mean that we can't reopen it. I will never stop working on this case," he told me with disappointment in his voice. True to his word, even five years later, he has continued to search for new avenues. His latest was getting cell phone records from anyone who was using their cell phone in the accident vicinity during that time period. He has done everything he could to solve it, but maybe it just wasn't meant to be. I actually felt relief. Whether that person was under the influence, texting, had a medical emergency, or hit Bryan on purpose, the person chose to leave the scene. Even if they didn't realize they hit someone, the next day they would have seen the damage to the car or seen a news story about it. They still chose not to come forward. This is a person I don't ever want to meet face to face. The slap on the wrist they would get if they went to court would just be an insult. Any money we would be awarded would not change the trauma they caused our family. There is one person who knows, and He will be the judge.

According to the Limited Crash Reconstruction Report conducted by the Minnesota State Patrol, with lack of tangible evidence, they did not or could not conclude how fast the vehicle or Bryan was traveling upon impact. There were no usual signs left at the accident scene. There were no skid marks that could help identify the type of vehicle on the basis of the tire or determine the speed of the vehicle involved. There were no obvious or substantial pieces of vehicle debris. Bryan tried to mentally recreate the accident, but nothing was adding up. Everything was in his favor such as a larger shoulder, sun at his back, a really long stretch of straight road, perfect weather. He only came up with two possible conclusions: first, a distracted driver or, second, a personal attack from someone who does not like cyclists on roads.

One night when we were out to dinner with our friend Rich, we started talking about the accident. We told him that we had no information about what happened. He suggested, "You should contact someone at Trek or Specialized bike company. There must be engineers that could look at Bryan's bike and determine how fast the vehicle was going when it hit Bryan by looking at where his bike snapped. The engineers have to conduct structural failure tests to determine how much pressure or impact a bike can take before it breaks."

We had never thought about doing this. As luck would have it, we have a family friend Laine that used to work at Trek as a mechanical/process engineer. I contacted him to see if he would be willing or if he knew of someone who would be willing to look at Bryan's bike and give us any information about what occurred. Laine connected us with one of his friends Todd who he felt was more qualified to do what we were asking. Todd agreed to look at all the data we had from the Minnesota State Patrol report. He also needed additional information: Bryan's height, weight, height of his bike, the extent of his injuries, size of bike wheel, weather conditions at the time of the accident, approximately how fast Bryan thought he was traveling, along with pictures of the bike from all angles.

Todd's report was an educated look at the forces and motion that Bryan's body and bicycle went through. He calculated that "Bryan traveled between seventy-one and one hundred seventeen miles per hour after impact. The bicycle damage and physical bodily injury damage suggests a very high G force acceleration (a sudden change of velocity). Based on how Bryan's bike was broken and the location of injuries to Bryan's body suggests the vehicle had a bumper clearance around eighteen inches. The bumper had to be high enough to clear the chain stays and hit the disc brake, forcing the wheel out of the bottom of the bike. The lack of plastic and paint flakes at the scene suggests that the impact was made with steel."

Bryan comprehended the physics and engineering in the analysis by Todd, which supported some of the ideas on what happened. However, he still is not closer to determining why it happened. As of now, we are not likely to ever get those questions answered.

When someone goes through an unexpected event, one always wonders, "How can I help?" My advice—show up! Don't ask what you can do for someone; just do something. Your act of kindness means so much. So many people stepped up for us. No act of kindness is too small. Something as simple as a card meant the world. My family couldn't have made it through without others. This has made me much more aware of what people are going through around me. When an accident happens or someone is first diagnosed with cancer, everyone rushes in right away to help. But after a short time, they go back to their lives while that person/family is still living in their nightmare. I have really tried to support people for the long haul, sending a card of encouragement, making them dinner, or getting a little gift. I want them to know that they aren't alone and I haven't forgotten about them.

Bryan and I have been asked to speak to a number of groups about different aspects of our journey. There have been several times that North Memorial Hospital has asked us to come back and share our experiences there. They are always wanting to improve the quality of care for their patients. We even had the privilege to participate in the virtual Lobby Day for Trauma Centers of America (TCAA). It was a chance to share our story of trauma with senators and representatives in Washington to advocate for more funding for trauma centers in the United States. Shani has asked me to come and be on a panel for her physical therapy students to talk about the caregiver role I was thrust into during Bryan's recovery. A boy scout troop asked Bryan to come and speak about bike safety and perseverance. We brought Bryan's bike to have reality hit home for the troop. Helmets not only save lives, but help prevent traumatic brain injuries. Bryan is living proof. Our church made a video of us telling our story in hopes of showing people the power of faith and compassion for others. We were honored to be a part of CaringBridge's twentieth anniversary. We were one of twenty people who got to work with David McLain, a National Geographic photojournalist, in a series he called "How We Heal."

Donating blood is something for which we still strongly advocate. I try to donate every fifty-six days. Bryan donates a few times a year only because his doctor doesn't want him to donate more than that. Unfortunately in 2022, Bryan got a blood clot in his lung. While on blood thinners, he had to stop donating. Since they can't determine a cause, he will more than likely have to be on a blood thinner for the rest of his life, which would end his ability to be a blood donor. Blood donations are one of the many reasons Bryan is still with us. He received over fifty units of blood and blood products. One doesn't realize how one trauma can use so much blood. That doesn't even account for the blood that is used on a daily basis for some patients. The Red Cross even tells you where your blood was sent, validating that you made a difference. In 2022, Bryan's story was used for a Red Cross flier. The flier was sent to O-negative donors to try to encourage them to donate more since they are universal donors.

People were so generous to us; we wanted to pay it forward. Therefore, we set up an account for that purpose, our version of a scholarship. We were so touched when strangers felt compelled to lift us up. So each year, we try to find someone in our community who has been involved in an accident and is going through a similar experience as our family did to donate to. We gave it to a high school student in the neighboring town who had an accident in his pool that left him paralyzed. Another year, we gave to a local family whose young adult children were involved in a horrific car accident. Their son died, and their daughter was severely injured with brain trauma and a broken pelvis. Previous to the car accident, I had been a client of the family's business. Unfortunately, they lost that too due to Covid. We wish no one would have to endure tragedy and pain. This past year, we donated to another Eagan family. The father crashed while mountain biking, suffering a traumatic brain injury. We hope these unexpected gifts are a beacon of hope through the darkness.

This experience created a new memory for us that will never be forgotten but really not the happiest. It drove home that, no matter how careful and safe you are, there are events that happen that are out of your control. Maximizing the happy memories and just remaining happy became one of our priorities. You can never prepare for events that can dramatically change your life. Once Bryan was out of the hospital and gaining strength, we could start building our libraries of happy memories through new adventures again. The generosity of our network of people connected to us was still coming in. We were given some incredible opportunities to help us get started. As life-long Packer fans, we were gifted front row tickets to the Packer vs. Bears game by the Look family. The seats were so good, Griffin and I made it on ESPN's live pregame broadcast. Griffin looking as cute as ever with his cheese head on was the perfect model for a crowd shot! The texts started coming in that night, "Hey, was that you on ESPN?" We had a great new memory and story to talk about finally instead of "the accident." Gin, a family friend, offered us use of her timeshare for a week anywhere we wanted to go. We chose to go to Arizona where we experienced the splendor of the Grand Canyon and Sedona. It was an amazing place and created another happy memory for the mental vault! Huge steps toward enjoying life and living it to the fullest.

As I write this, the world is going through a global pandemic. The ICU beds are full, there are no visitors, or visiting hours are limited for people to see someone in the hospital. I hate to think about what would have happened if Bryan's accident had occurred now. Would they have fought so hard to keep him alive? They may have needed the ventilator for someone else. Would there have even been a bed for him? I would not have been allowed to stay with him like I did. I can't imagine only seeing Bryan for three hours a day or less. Not knowing what was happening the other twenty-one hours would have been agony. It breaks my heart to think about someone being all alone fighting for their life and watching videos of people saying goodbye to their loved ones over FaceTime.

Dr. Beal told us many times, "Bryan, you were strong when you came in here. And you will be strong again." Bryan definitely took the long way home, but here we are six years later, JoasStrong, and more resilient than ever.

A Few Words from Bryan

Thank You

I can't express how grateful I am for everyone's contributions to the ultimate happily-ever-after ending of the story. It was a scary and uncertain time. Thank you for the amazing outpouring of love and generosity given to my family and me. Thank you for the consideration everyone showed by providing gifts and activities for our children. It was beyond belief. Thank you to my wonderful in-laws who were on their way south for a spring road trip but canceled their vacation and turned around to come back and care for our kids. This allowed Shauna to spend her time with me at the hospital, which was too far away for a reasonable daily commute. Thank you to all the nurses, doctors, and rest of the staff at North Memorial for taking such good care of me. Thank you to the University of Minnesota 2016 Lacrosse team for giving my son a birthday he will never forget. This list goes on. Most of the events happened when I had no comprehension of what was going on. I only learned through stories after my brain came back on line. One of the first memories was mustering the energy of signing my name to all the thank-you cards Shauna wrote up. There were a lot!

Cycling is a passion

Early in my life, my father introduced me to the sport of cycling. The idea was that it was fun and provided freedom for adventure. My competitiveness soon took over by the age of fourteen, and I wanted to take my riding to the next level and race. Bike racing was very uncommon in my community. I only knew of Greg LeMond and the Tour de France. I started by timing myself on routes that I would ride over and over again trying to achieve a faster time. I remember calculating my average speed in eighth grade algebra class. I then started to seek out bike races. I found one that was in Prescott, Wisconsin. I made a few contacts after the race and got a lot of advice about equipment and ways to get more involved.

This hobby has generated many good friendships and memories over the years. The health benefits that I have accumulated over thirty years of cycling, I believe, greatly helped my body to physically recover from the accident to the condition I am currently in. However, I am not sure I'll ever be as cycling strong as I once was. The many "epic" rides I've been on helped my mental perseverance and taught me how to suffer until the ride or event was over. A recent quote by world road race champion, Julian Alaphilippe, sums it up best: "There is a very big mental part; that's undeniable. You have to like to suffer to win races and you have to be able to dig deep into the pain to do big things. You have to be a masochist to ride a bike. It's such a difficult sport." We would be over a hundred miles into a ride in the middle of nowhere, and the only solution was to put your head down and pedal to get home. There were times in the hospital that I just put my head down to suffer through to the end. I never internally panicked. I had some uncomfortable situations that I had to get through that tested me, but I never had any real doubt that I couldn't get to the finish line of going home.

Spring of 2016

I was off to a good start on my cycling fitness. We were seeing an atypical warm Minnesota late winter/early spring. I was working on a good series of outdoor road rides and was excited to be outside training more. The Sunday before the accident, I met my good buddies, Mike, Gregg, and Jiggy in Danbury, Wisconsin, for a fifty-five-mile ride. The warm weather also meant that it was time to start riding my bike to work, which I had been progressively doing more and more of over the previous five years. Not only was it good for the environment and saving money on gas, I used it as a method to build riding time into my schedule. If I rode to work, it was much easier to take a long route home since I was already on my bike. If I drove to work, it seemed like I would never go for a ride once I got home. The Tuesday of the accident was another beautiful day in a string of warm days. The major issue with early spring riding is daylight. I typically never ride at night. I was able to leave work around 4 p.m. so I could finish a longer ride home before dark. One of my regular routes was to head south from my office to get to roads that generally have light traffic. This is one of the more ironic things about the accident. I have ridden thousands of miles over my thirty years of riding, and I had never been hit by a car or really had any close calls. I might expect a lapse at an interaction where a driver missed a stop sign or didn't see me, which is why I would rate it as one of the safest roads I ride on. However, I did discover one flaw of this road with no traffic, which was there were no witnesses. Lucky for me, I was fortunate that a few people stopped when they saw my bike in the road. Their simple actions were the first of many that ultimately saved my life.

I have no memory of what happened. I remember, or think I remember, riding up to the time before the accident. However, since I have ridden that route so many times, I am not sure if the memories are real or something my mind pieced together from previous rides. This has been one of the more difficult facts to deal with, not knowing what happened. I can only guess what

I would have done. Hit and lying in the ditch, I would have expected myself to pull my phone from my jersey pocket and call Shauna for a "bail out." I had done this numerous times for thunderstorms, bad mechanicals, or one time on a hundred-mile ride when I thought I was too dehydrated to finish my ride home. However, the reports state my phone was not in my pocket when I was found, so that was not an option. My pelvis was broken, along with fractured vertebrae, and internal bleeding, so I could not have flagged down traffic to find help. Here is the biggest PSA (public service announcement)—my head turned out to be perfectly fine thanks to my helmet. The people that found me shared with me that I was lucid and verbal but quickly going into shock. There may have been a chance I was trying to take the steps to call for help. The emergency vehicles responded only to determine that I needed Level 1 trauma care, and they were not going to be able to transport me in time. Lucky for me, it was time for my first helicopter ride! Bummer I have no memory of it.

The next "day" (actually three weeks later), I began to wake up. I had many dreams and visions that mixed with reality. The first "memory" I had was that I was on a boat because the hospital was full. The only way out was behind me. I thought there was a bathroom there, so I tried to think of ways to get toward the bathroom to escape the boat and get out. It was my understanding I needed to "wait my turn." In that memory, there was also another person lying on top of me, in my bed, that was in worse shape. I am not sure if this was the medical equipment on me or the fact my pelvis was broken and I just couldn't move. I did not understand what was wrong other than I needed to wait. I had no pain or any suffering going on in these memories. That state of reality turned into a desire to leave the hospital, which stayed with me until the bitter end. I was convinced that, if I could just get to my own bed, I only needed a day or two of rest to be back to normal. I started to think through other plans to escape in my dreams. At one point "on the boat," my college roommate, Stewy, came to visit me. I would describe him as more of a "city boy" than me, so when he told me he bought an ass (aka, donkey), it proved to me that I was actually dreaming. The boat could be real, but Stewy owning a donkey? What kind of medication was I on to have hallucinations such as this? Even crazier, it was later confirmed to be true, so I wasn't imagining everything during this time. I did process the information correctly, and they were donkey owners! The "extra patient" in my room eventually left, although I am not sure where they went. That part of the dream was proven false.

Then my reality morphed into being in a mall-like environment. The ICU was shaped like a "U" with the nurses' station in the center. I saw other "stores" or "kiosks," which I assume were the other patient rooms, open and close daily, all while I was still waiting for someone to come help me. In the center of the mall, there was a bubbly drink machine that served root beer and lemonade. Next to the bubbly drink machine was the Minnesota State Fair butter sculpture, which I have never seen in person. Why that was in my current reality, I have no idea, as we rarely attend the Minnesota Great Get-Together. Every day, the mall would open and close, and no one would help me. It was somewhat agonizing, but I was still in a peaceful place.

I slowly started to recognize people. The only thing I wanted to do was go home. I tried to enlist the help of anyone I could to break me out of there. I just needed to rub some dirt on it and get back on the bike. I have crashed my bike many times in my life. You ordinarily end up with lots of shallow abrasions—road rash. You have to clean out the embedded dirt and rocks. The worst injury I had received from a crash was a cut that maybe needed some stitches. The healing process was always painful, but you fight through it. That was what a tough rider did. Look at what the Tour de France riders go through. They are professionals but they are crashing all the time and most continue to carry on in the race. No one seemed willing to let me go home, making it start to set in that I was not OK. I needed to concentrate on rest and begin the recovery.

One of my first requests was for a root beer float. As Shauna had mentioned, it was a bit of a shock to her, since I rarely ever drank root beer and certainly wouldn't be the first beverage I would have asked for. She and everyone else was unaware of the vision and torture of watching root beer being served every day. The respiratory therapist delivered. But, like everything else, my vision of how the root beer would taste was much different than reality. I think I only ended up taking a couple of sips, foreshadowing the difficult transition back to real food and drink would be.

The recovery process was draining. I was never really in pain. The energy to make basic movements was overwhelming. And it all started with the basic activity of breathing. After being intubated for fourteen days, I had to have a tracheotomy, which meant I was breathing out of a tube in my throat. I couldn't talk and getting oxygen was a chore. I had to concentrate so hard on breathing that I thought, if I fell asleep, I would not wake up again. This made going to sleep terrifying. I would drift off and wake up in a panic gasping for breath, thinking I had slept for eight hours, but it ended up being only five minutes. This happened over and over again. Actual sleep proved to be elusive throughout the hospital stay. The hospital is a busy place, with lots of activities and check-ins. Every time I thought I was going to meditate myself to sleep, something would interrupt me. I was still having various dreams and visions when I did finally get to sleep.

Early in my recovery process, one particular vision stands out. I was under water, and there were neon lights all around me lit up with a black light like at a dance club. In the middle of the water was a giant sea anemone. It was a big oval with a blue center and a pink ring around it with about one hundred small tentacles. It was telling me, "You need to die to save all the jellyfish. You've done enough. Now it is time to leave. Just come with me. You will pass and be at peace." For whatever reason, that anemone was making a very persuasive argument. I am not sure that if I had actually followed the sea anemone I would not have woken up. I remember thinking I was not ready to die. Then I woke up. This dream or vision seemed more real than the rest of the dreams I had while sleeping and also added to the anxiety of falling asleep. After that dream, future dreams were less dramatic even though I still continued to find it difficult to sleep on a set schedule or for a full night.

Once breathing became a natural reflex again, I thought I could focus on some other items. Maybe I could catch up on some reading or watch movies. However, I never felt like I was ever able to fully relax. Anytime I tried to concentrate on a story line, I struggled to mentally keep focused. I did seem to watch a lot of episodes of *American Pickers*, which were short and had no real storyline to follow. I was convinced that my issue was that the hospital was not a restful place and I needed to get home.

My children did visit on Sundays, but I was not really in a condition to interact with them for long. I loved seeing them, but I couldn't move very well, so I just lay there. Not too exciting. I was grateful that they were super busy with school and activities and were being taken care of so they didn't need to come see me that often. I wanted to be able to go home to see them rather than them coming to the hospital to see me. That argument I continued to lose, but I don't think anyone thought it would take eighty-eight days.

I am thankful that Shauna kept a CaringBridge site as a record of the events that happened. I have blips of memories, but it wasn't until around week eight that I had any lasting memories. It is incredible to go back and read everything I went through.

Even after getting home, it was a long and slow recovery. I was requested not to stand until my acetabulum (hip sockets) healed, which did not check out until July 6, 2016. I lost so much strength during this time of immobility, my training turned into physical therapy. I was eager to get back to work full time and to ride my bike. I eased back into work; the hard part was being able to stay focused all day.

Mike talked me into buying a fat-tire bike to ride in the snow. Mike, Gregg, and I met up north in Duluth to ride the trails in the fall right after the bikes came in. I was feeling OK but still so weak. Halfway through the ride, I was spent and split off from the other two to noodle my way back to the cars at my own pace. The trails are outstanding in that area and also very hilly. The trail I was on had a few wooden bridges to cross small gaps. One of those gaps was a steep slope up, and I did not have the power to make it up the bridge. With my feet clipped in the pedals, I came to a stop on the slope and slowly tipped over into the ravine. This has happened before, and it feels like you are going in slow motion. I could only begin to wonder how my body was going to do with the impact. Luckily, it was a soft landing. The only bruise was to my ego as I remounted, realizing how long it was going to take to be close in strength to where I was before the accident.

I continued to train indoors most of the winter, and just over a year after the accident, I was able to complete a sixty-mile gravel bike ride with Mike and Gregg. I was still slow and weak but ecstatic I could do something like that again. I was already thinking about how I could adjust and train to go faster the following year. I may never get back to the same level, but I still have a passion for riding my bike and enjoying the time with my friends on those adventures that I look forward to going on for many years to come.

I am blessed that I came out on the other side of a horrific situation and got a second chance to watch my children grow up, enjoy my time with my wife, and return to normal life activities. The support through this dark time was not something I imagined I would ever need in my lifetime. From the people that discovered me, to the first responders, to the surgeons, nurses, therapists, to family and friends, to total strangers that all provided the help when I really needed it—I was humbled by everything that happened during this experience. You can't always just put your head down to get to the finish line in life on your own without help.

Acknowledgements

Writing has been something that has always been my nemesis. But there was something in me that compelled me to tell our story. Not only will it be a record of our story, but hopefully an inspiration for those who read it.

To Bryan ~ thank you for allowing me to tell our story, the good, the bad, and the ugly. You are a living miracle. There is something more you were meant to do. I am behind you every step of the way.

To my children, Griffin and Elyse ~ you may not even realize the traumatic experience you went through, but you were champions through it all. You learned first-hand how to help and support others in a time of crisis. My hope for you is that you pay that forward.

To my parents, Jim and Lou Ann ~ you have always been there for me and put family first. You stopped your lives to take care of my babies. Your unconditional love and encouragement made it possible for me to concentrate on all decisions for Bryan and his recovery. Mom, you spent many hours helping me get my words onto paper to make this book possible.

To my sister, Erica, and my nieces, Morgan and Ingrid ~ every chance you had, you came to visit. Erica, you took a day off of school every week to come and spend the day with me.

To my inner circle, Shani and Mike, Shelly and Gregg, Stewy, Greg, Angie, Jenny, Jaleh, Catherine, Kathy and Bill, Carmen and John, Jill, Pastor Kris ~ you are the ones that were with me on my darkest days. You made it possible for me to breathe and keep going.

To the doctors, nurses, therapists, and the entire staff of North Memorial Hospital ~ your knowledge and care for Bryan was beyond measure. You worked tirelessly to put Bryan back together again. You treated me and my family with compassion during our ordeal.

To our coworkers at Red Pine and MHC Company ~ not only did you keep our jobs going until we could come back, you supported us by donating meals/money, hosting blood drives, and innumerable other things.

To Alexa and Tony and the other good Samaritans ~ thank you for stopping to help Bryan. Your quick actions got Bryan the help he needed as soon as possible. It is comforting to know that people were surrounding him with prayers and love before I even knew he was in an accident.

To Bryan's parents, Steve and Jan ~ thank you for coming when you could and getting the temporary shower on the main level ready for Bryan while dealing with the progression of Jan's dementia, which she ultimately passed away from on May 15, 2021.

To the 2016 men's Gopher lacrosse team ~ thank you for making Griffin have an extra-special birthday. Your kindness meant the world to a ten-year-old boy.

To our Walnut Ridge Neighborhood ~ we are so grateful to live in a neighborhood where you took care of all the things around our house.

To Griffin's Squirt C team ~ thank you for our yard spring clean-up and all the support you offered.

To Elyse's U8 girls' hockey team and EHA (Eagan Hockey Association) ~ thank you for hosting a skating and root beer float fundraiser. The support of the hockey community was remarkable.

To Nate ~ thank you for your musical talents in producing a fundraising concert in our hometown of Chippewa Falls, Wisconsin.

To Mike Akan and his band, and Jon and Jess Joles ~ thank you for your time and talents at the JoasStrong FUNdraiser. It was a great night of fun and music.

To my editor, Kate ~ you were instrumental in guiding and questioning me to help me explore and stretch my story to be what it is today.

To Detective Fitzgerald ~ thank you for your relentless pursuit in following every lead to try and find the person responsible for hitting Bryan.

To the family, friends, and strangers that held us up and supported us ~ thank you for delivering meals, sending cards, donating prizes for and attending fundraisers, giving blood, writing words of encouragement, and countless other gestures bestowed upon us. Know your actions will always remain in our hearts. It didn't go unnoticed. We wouldn't have made it through without you all.

Remember to live life. You never know what the future holds. Don't take your loved ones for granted. Don't be distracted when you drive. Be kind—you might need it returned to you someday. Thank you for being on this journey with us. We are #JoasStrong.

Kids Racing

Bryan racing

Bryan's bike he was riding

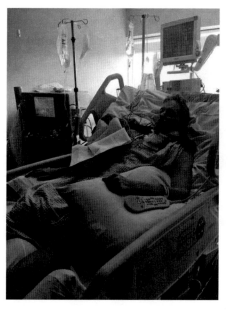

First picture of Bryan in hospital

ICU family area

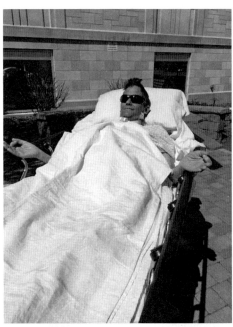

Escaping the ICU for some sun

Dr. Beal

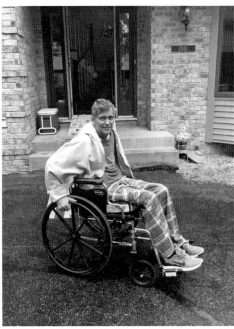

Finally Home after 88 days

JoasStrong family picture

On the Today Show

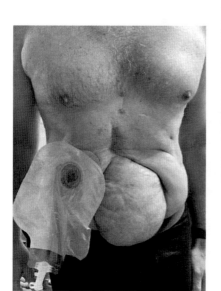

Bryan's abdomen today

Joas Family 2022

The JoasStrong logo

Bryan riding his bike on the road the accident took place.

Bryan was found near the big tree.